Celebrate Yourself

Celebrate Yourself

The Secret to a Life of Hope and Joy

by Bryan Jay Cannon

Word Books, Publisher

Waco, Texas

First Printing—May 1977
Second Printing—August 1977

ISBN: 0-87680-802-X
Library of Congress catalog card number: 76-48542

Printed in the United States of America

Contents

Preface

Acknowledgments

Chapter 1   Is Your Life Worth Celebrating?   13

Chapter 2   The Joy of Breaking Out........   19

Chapter 3   Can You Celebrate Yourself?....   27

Chapter 4   How Can We Celebrate,
Feeling As We Do?.............   39

Chapter 5   Celebrate Your Sexuality.......   49

Chapter 6   Rejoicing in Your Brother......   63

Chapter 7   Celebration Through
Preferring Others..............   71

Chapter 8   Can Suffering Be a Cause
to Celebrate?....................   81

Chapter 9   Celebrating Life Even
Facing Death   91

Chapter 10   Celebrating History............   99

Chapter 11   A Celebrating Community   107

Chapter 12   Does It Really Work?   117

Notes   125

Study Guide.................................   129

Preface

There has been no single discovery I've made about life and people more important than this—contrary to what we have often heard, most people do not have too high a regard toward themselves. Most people do not like themselves enough. Life just isn't that great, and their own lives don't seem worthy of talking about celebrating. Sitting down and getting into what they really feel about themselves reveals many reasons why people do not have a high regard for themselves. Life *isn't* worth celebrating for them. I know what that's like.

In the last decade of my life I have been to the heights and the depths. I've felt tremendously successful as a person and as a professional, and I've felt a total failure as both. And I've grown older. I'm not the flippant young enthusiast who speaks in the glowing absolutes that have preceded disappointment for so many hopeful people where the promises don't measure up to the practice.

There is a new and deep gratitude and satisfaction that is working in me, and it has come through trial and error and trial by fire. But I *know* my life is worth celebrating, and if mine is, so is yours. This is what I have to share.

BRYAN JAY CANNON

Acknowledgments

I celebrate all those in whom I have rediscovered my real self and life as God meant it to be. Special gratitude goes to Elizabeth Sloat for grammatical help and Marjorie Heiberger, Gertrude Gross and Jane Waller for patiently typing and retyping the manuscript, and my loving and patient wife, Phyllis, for proof-reading and advice.

1

Is Your Life Worth Celebrating?

Some time ago I went away for a week, and with six other people spent the time in deep evaluation of myself. One of the conclusions at which I arrived was that I was a composite of the expectations of everyone else—my church, my family, society, my parental programing. But where was the real me?

I could identify with C.S. Lewis when, just evolving into a whole person, he could only recall, "When I remember my outer life, I see clearly that the other is but momentary flashes, seconds of gold scattered in months of dross, each instantly swallowed up in the old, familiar, sordid, hopeless weariness . . . merely a coarse curtain which at any moment might be drawn aside to reveal all the weariness I then knew." [1] This duality—flecks of joy against the seemingly endless backdrop of normal daily life—can jade your thinking. It has mine, but I'm changing. Yet I wouldn't blame you if you didn't even want to read further, bitter from disenchantment and unfulfilled promises. Still, deep inside each of us, inside of *you,* is something unique and marvelous. More exciting still is that it is still seeking to be known. If you have not known that *something,* alive and free, if you haven't felt "filled by the Holy Spirit" to grow and enjoy, then struggle with me to understand something which is difficult to put into words. Jean-Paul Sartre said, "The ultimate evil is to turn what is concrete into an abstraction." Every attempt here will be to keep this struggle from abstractions, for too often people have confided in me that they have found the Christian faith to be abstract words. Possibly we haven't actually thought it out, but the feeling we have is, "How does it all make sense to *me* in *my* daily life?"

What we need is something which God intended for us to experience within ourselves as natural. "Celebration," Ross Snyder says, "is a life of style. It isn't what we do. It is what we *are* which has caught the integrity of nature and the universe and is on-its-way-to-wholeness. The Greek word is *hilaritas*, a word used for centuries in the Christian community to name a life which could be given the name 'courage enjoying being a freedom'." [2] Celebration is acting out publicly what we are, an expression of our wholeness.

We choose our life-style. I've realized how I have done this. For instance, my life has been so crowded, my schedule so demanding sometimes. Yet I would accept responsibilities, speaking engagements, program demands that further complicated my life. Then I would burn myself out trying to do it all, nobly saying I had to because of my schedule. But I chose it, and out of it all I often lost my joy! But I chose my style by the decisions I made along the way. Others also let life happen to them, and they are really institutionalized, imprisoned in ideas and responsibilities so they end up victimized by themselves. We can choose to allow our spontaneity to die, to suffocate our flame, to resist the Holy Spirit and not pursue mystery and joy, or we can choose *hilaritas!* I'm now systematically changing my life-style, my schedule, and my attitude to be "courage enjoying being a freedom." A poster describes what I expect our life together as the church to be in the world—"Celebration is a million candles lit with reverence and joy." Isn't that great? That is the description I want for all our activities in our church—our training, worship and service, toward the end of turning on the lives of one another and the world with reverence and joy! You and I need to celebrate ourselves with all our feelings and being, all of our relationships, for that to become a reality. Wouldn't that be great if we could? If we only would!

A few friends went out to lunch some time ago to celebrate the birthday of one of the group. But the one celebrating most was not the man having the birthday. It was the one who had set up the luncheon. If I ever knew someone turned on, Frank is. Frank has started to live. He told us, "I used to go to church and come dragging out, filled with guilt and unhappy about life. Since I have been coming here, I am so happy I could bust. I'm alive. I find out I'm somebody . . . God's somebody! I have worth. I count! And because of this, I care. I really feel I live for others now, because I can enjoy myself." All of this after just coming out of a hospital bed a couple of weeks before from a heart attack. Incidentally, because of his life, the interns and the doctor's lives were challenged and dramatically influenced. How did this happen? An ordinary draftsman had heard only a reverse gospel in the past. It had been bad news of how sinful he was. He was unable to shape up like he had been bombarded to do in his previous church experience and was very unhappy. He floated on becalmed seas without either wind or sail.

Somehow, in the marvelous mystery of the Holy Spirit's movement, Frank was able to hear what I find most people have not been able to really hear in terms of their own personhood. Frank discovered he was a very special person, like everyone of us is before God. His problem was not his sin. Christianity believes Jesus took care of man's sin in his death for each one of us. Frank's problem was his response to God's wonderful action in Jesus' death. If prison doors have been unlocked and have swung open for you and you still hide in the corner of the dark cell or bang your head against the damp cell wall, the light of freedom will never be yours. You have to walk out and stretch, rub your eyes, and claim your freedom. Frank is beginning to discover how to respond. And life is celebration for him in almost every situation in which he finds himself, even in a hospital with a heart attack. Because this is true, others are learning to celebrate their own lives in the splash-over!

Our ability to discover this freedom is affected by those around us. This truth became vividly clear in a sensitivity group in which we were seeking to learn how to be more authentic and honest. A sharp young woman remarked about the difficulty she was having with her husband, who is a professional churchman. He constantly criticized her. She couldn't seem to do anything right. She especially felt this was more pronounced when he was under pressure in his work, but even so she seldom felt affirmed. Yet she had a radiant face and philosophy of life, even though her Christianity seemed thin in terms of orthodox doctrine. She believed that one of the most basic dimensions of the Christian life was to be truly human, to come to grips with who you are and to take each situation and see what you can make of it. She tried to meet each person and see where there was some goodness in him. She loved life and people. She was in the therapy group to know herself better so she could have more to offer her husband and others. When she asked us what we thought of her, we saw her differently than she saw herself. We agreed that what was coming across to us was not the shy, inadequate person she thought she was. Rather, to us she was a very positive, alive, and vivacious Christian woman, one who undoubtedly was a threat to her proper, plodding, uptight husband. His recourse had been to project his own anxiety on her and make her feel guilty because of it. The problem was in him, not her. She was celebrating, and he wasn't in on it!

The church has not always communicated an attitude of celebration either. All too often the church has projected its own uptightness as much as that husband did on his wife, over the ages leaving a feeling in so many that life is not celebration but drudgery. We have gotten the idea that man is not a divinely created opportunity for joyous work, worship, and winsomeness, but a tragic failure. That's what "You are a sinner" often communicates. However, it was not an accident that Christianity began with angels singing, *Joy to the world!* Our Master came announcing he wanted us to have life abundant, and joy would be with us and in us. The record is quite clear. There is more to life than most of us claim. Jesus showed his power first at a party—a wedding feast. Paul, transformed by divine shock treatment from a legalistic scalp-hunter running down heretics to someone who writes that tremendous thirteenth chapter of 1 Corinthians on love, dots his writing with desire for others to have the joy he has had. It was joy, incidentally, under some of the most trying, painful, threatening situations possible.

Some miss this dimension of Paul's writings. There is a zest for life, a sparkle, a validation for living which speaks of celebration. It outshines and outlasts any of the artificial stimulants so many people are using today to try to expand consciousness and awareness. It contradicts tight-lipped, sad-faced, puritanical Christianity more than other supposed enemies of the faith. It is an aliveness, a healthy awareness which we are to celebrate in ourselves, in one another, and in God's world. Celebrating that way makes sense to us—how we will glorify God and enjoy him forever! If blacks think they are beautiful . . . and they are . . . what is each of us as a beautiful creature of God to think of ourselves and one another?

We cannot expect simple little answers to deep, eternal questions which involve the whole complex nature of our human personality and the world about us. Life is the continuing experience of knowing yourself as the unique person the Eternal God created you to be at any given moment, with destiny and purpose, in a marvelous union with his Spirit. The setting is a real world filled with problems and tough challenges. But most of us are such a hodge-podge of components, pieced together patches of everyone else's designs, there is little wonder we have difficulty knowing, let alone celebrating, ourselves. What we do know sometimes hurts! We are what our parents wanted us to be, or forced —knowingly or unknowingly—on us. We are composites of ideas, inhibitions, patterns of thoughts our teachers pressed into our pliable forming personalities as children. We are partially the fears and worries, failures and mistakes of our society we have picked up. We are certainly partly made up of our responses to the pressure of structures and groups of which we are presently a part. Our jobs, our community, our church, our country, and most certainly, our family are all part of it. These components of our being are held together with the important rules, routines, and responsibilities of daily life. Some are good and noble. Some are also questionable and hypocritical. There are dishonest demands, threats, and intimidations in our culture which have helped mold every one of us.

Maybe we need to periodically reevaluate who we are and where we are going, and what our lives at that moment mean.

On vacation, stretched in the southern sand and sun, a hard-hitting industrial executive told me, "All my life I have driven myself. There was no fun in living. I fought and scratched to make it to the top. Now I am finding I'm back-filling in all the areas I missed along the way." It has been about ten years since he too discovered Christ, who had a gift to give him. Eight years ago, I had asked him where he wanted to be in ten years. He decided his values and goals were inconsistent with the gift of God's grace he had received previously. Those ten years have passed. Now he is celebrating himself, others, his Lord's world—life! Paul's promise at the end of 1 Thessalonians 5 is enlightening, "He who calls you is faithful, and he will do it." If you don't get in the way, Christ will do it in and through you!

What a life there is to live! What an experience we can have within ourselves, in others around us, in this marvelous world, and in dimensions of the Spirit we haven't begun to understand and claim! *Christ will do it if you will let him.* Respond! Rejoice always! Let's celebrate! How? I believe it is in acknowledging that we are important, that we have value and worth, that life was meant to have meaning and purpose, and that it can be a celebration experience. Believe with me!

2

The Joy of Breaking Out

As a youngster I wanted to be more free than I felt my parents allowed. I hated restraint. By nature I kept trying to "get out," even when I was very small, and it meant crawling over the gate on the porch.

I suppose it isn't unnatural. Children are always seeking more freedom. But as I got older it was deeper than that. For me it was an internal struggle regarding my personhood, the integrity of claiming my own individuality, to be *me*. So it has finally dawned on me that I have been searching for a breakthrough for a long time. I see the same search in my oldest children, and I'm not convinced they haven't inherited something from their dad!

In my search I would never have thought the answer had anything to do with being a Christian. Although I thought deeply about religious questions long before I took the church seriously, that was not at all the direction of my search for freedom. Take the matter of being a "good" Christian.

I like to ask people this question—When they think of being good or of being a "good" Christian, do they think of the term *freedom?* Invariably the response is negative. Rather, they think of a restricted life, hedged with rules, encumbered with duties, and restricted by a specific image of what is proper.

But that is so different from Jesus! I sometimes feel we

19

would be very uncomfortable having Jesus as a companion, for sometimes he *broke* the rules! Why, he said that the Sabbath was made for men to enjoy, to be refreshed and restored. Man wasn't made for the Sabbath! Jesus violated protocol and good manners, eating with "unclean hands." He fractured the safe, tight conformity of his community's codes, picking grain to eat on the Sabbath. He kept the wrong company; he ate with those who ate too much. He drank with those who drank too much. He partied with party people and ended with a reputation inconsistent with the image of someone religious. Someone even tried labeling him a glutton and a drunkard.

Most of the pictures we have of Jesus have been of a somber, bathrobed fellow, rather strange and different from us, caring for sheep and little children.

In a previous book I have described an original sketch I cherish by artist Richard Hook.[1] The first time I saw it I realized I must own this picture, for it was such a great contrast to the rather effeminate, sterile portrayals of Jesus I'd seen. This one shows a rugged, virile fellow walking up from the shore with his arms around the shoulders of two men who are dressed in the simple garb of fishermen. There are smiles on their faces, mixed with the expectancy of comradeship born for adventure, joy of hoped-for freedom. Over the shoulder of Jesus are two other fishermen, trailing behind and looking on. On their faces is this—"What am I missing? I wish I could get in on that!"

Maybe that is the unconscious wish of most of us. Possibly we have trailed along behind, not ever having sensed that utter acceptance of Jesus (let alone acceptance by others). We have felt we have not had his touch, his call, his freeing acceptance, the abandonment of adventure with him. Possibly one of the reasons we are at once supportive and repressive to our young people is that age and social awareness have not yet repressed their spontaneity as it often does ours. It might just be that one of the reasons good and sober saints look with great suspicion on freakish dress and hangouts which provide wild music for the kids is not that there might be drugs present. It is because the style is different, non-conforming, abandoned like we once were when we were young.

Do you remember . . . ? Do you remember . . . ?

What do we do to each other, pressing ourselves into safely handled stereotypes? The truth of the matter is if we can find some characteristic, some personality trait, especially some sin or failure with which to type a person, this is the image that remains with us. Then we do not have to deal with that individual as a dynamic personality, to be newly encountered and received and understood each time. This is partly the reason we hide our true selves, allowing others to only know what is safe, the attitudes and actions easily merchandised in social intercourse. For you see, we might be otherwise identified as "that" kind of person. Yet, as someone wrote recently, in a pamphlet entitled, *This Is Faith At Work,* "The protective shells we build around us scarcely hide our inner restlessness. We go through life learning to play a variety of roles, but wondering who we really are and what is the purpose of it all. Traditional forms lose their meaning, and we grope for a reality that seems beyond our reach."

For me, I accepted the judgment and intimidation of others, of the world, of adulthood, so that much of the spontaneity, the adventure, the openness to new ways of feeling and new awareness to the meaning of living were repressed.

Now before I go on with some concrete suggestions, I have to admit that the older I become and the more I know myself, the more guarded I am in speaking in absolutes or in giving advice to others. So, I don't want to give advice here.

Also, as we know, freedom is a relative term. I have discovered that I am not yet free in areas of my being yet undiscovered, and in others recognized but still being processed. I often need to go back and reclaim God's freedom in areas I thought settled once and for all. I need the supportive correction and insight of a fellowship to keep me free. Therefore, understanding we are not speaking in unrealistic absolutes, think with me for a moment of what it might be to discover or recapture the joy of spontaneity in Jesus Christ and of learning to claim the same for others.

First of all, take a fresh look at an old and fundamental truth of our faith. One of the prison-houses for Christians is that while *we talk about living under grace,* as a matter of fact, *we live by works.* Our culture is built on a reward system. Being good deserves a reward. Merit reaps a better standing. And we have seen someone *trying* to be a free person. He usually stands out in the crowd as a phony, boorish in his blasé attitude, inconsiderate in his self-acquired, so-called freedom, sometimes embarrassing in his effort to be spontaneous.

I have had uptight people desiring a new kind of life tell me, "I've tried, but I can't seem to find personal freedom!" The key isn't in adopting some new style or program. It is in a Person! The key is in Christ. Paul put it simply, "For freedom *Christ* has set us free." It comes, not in trying, but in trusting him! That means living in a growing awareness of a vital relationship with Jesus Christ.

Others have told me, "I've done as much as the next person. I've been regular in church, trying to do what is right. . . ." But they are no different than I am. I've found every time I get into a compulsive, strained effort, the goal is elusive. For it isn't so much in *doing* as in *being.*

> Jesus Christ is Lord and HE has set me free. All the things I know about myself that pull me down have no hold over me any longer. All the failures, the habits, the inconsistencies, the weaknesses which are so difficult to overcome are powerless to encumber me. There's no telling the kind of person I might be, for I'm only what my Lord and I make of the stuff of life today, tomorrow, and each new day! The key is my being his, not doing . . . the key is my trusting, not trying . . . I'm Christ's freed person!

Program *that* into your life as a start and what might be the new edge of spontaneity in you!

Another point is as important as the first. *What we claim for ourselves, we can allow for others.* You might sit down before today runs out, think carefully of how you stereotype certain kinds of people. Then take a piece of paper, draw a line down the middle and list on one side exactly how you have done the very thing which has been the deadly trap of your own soul, writing down specific people and situations which you can recall. On the other side, try to analyze why you do it. For each situation or person, examine what in you might cause you to put people in categories. Make a new decision to experiment with relationships. Practice looking at friends and family in a new way. Imagine meeting them for the first time. Disregard information you have about them. Try to forget past experiences and stereotypes you have with a number of people —your husband or wife, boss, child, fellow employees. Think this: Jesus is now loving, accepting, listening, enabling through me.

As new as this kind of thought might be, don't dismiss it as far beyond you, or for that matter, far behind you! If you are a layman, I want you to know that if we meet and if we have a chance to relate, I do not intend to stereotype you as a "layman." I'll allow you to be whoever you dare to be, and I will pray for and support you. In the same way, I refuse to fulfill anyone's stereotype of a clergyman. I intend to be God's free man if I can and hope to break out of the prison of being stereotyped by others. Or for that matter, of stereotyping others myself!

Another important step I have found, especially in counseling, is *trusting ourselves to one other person with whom we can dare to be honest*. We have to be unapologetically frank to talk about our dreams and fantasies, our shattered hopes, even the "could-have-beens" we might have thought we filed away. If we are as real as possible, sometimes the Holy Spirit can speak most clearly in the echo of our own voice, bouncing off the understanding of a friend. Claim the freedom to be yourself as someone else knows, accepts, and enables you. We try to be that for each other on our church staff. But I also have a layman or two who are trusted friends with whom I can tell it like it is. It is one of my ways of staying honest.

One woman I talked with was so rigid, so unhappy and frigid, that every aspect of her life could be calculated— how she dressed, fixed her hair, would react to any given subject, even to the one brand of perfume she wore. She had become a joyless, perfunctory image you could calculate she would be today and tomorrow and next week. When I suggested she try to get in touch with some of the re- pressed, smothered dimensions of herself, she was almost frightened.

We talked about God giving her permission she never granted herself (and felt family, friends, the world never gave her) to experiment with some freedom and new feeling —a new hairstyle, a walk in the woods barefoot, lying on a hill and feeling the sun on her face, cotton candy and a ferris wheel, a frilly dress, lunch with a girl friend in the big city with no obligations and the expectancy of buying something for fun just for herself. It was almost too much. But she started to experiment, believing Christ loved her with an open edge to living, and the transformation was amazing!

So long as it is neither immoral nor harmful to someone, *do something you would like to do just for fun as a declaration of freedom.* Let it be "un-typical" for you, and do it boldly, in Jesus' name! For freedom, Christ HAS set you free!

I need to do this to reaffirm my freedom and individuality. My image as a pastor so often locks me into always reacting according to that image. I remember coming back from a meeting out of town. It was a beautiful sunny day and my heart was singing. I put the top down on my car, stripped to the waist, lit up a cigar and broke the image that locks me in so often. You might not think that's a very dramatic, daring thing. That's not the point. For me it was a very freeing experience. I shared this with a friend I see only occasionally, and then under rather formal situations. He says he thinks of that picture now when he thinks of me, and it is a reassurance to him of an open-endedness and spontaneity to life he needs to remember also.

I am finding there is a new kind of good feeling inside when I break out of the prisons I make for myself. When I do, I also become able to avoid stereotyping others. Spontaneity is then much more possible. I can begin to have fun in living, for I live on the creative edge of God's new thing for me.

A very remarkable experience happened in the fellowship hall of our church. Cecil Osborne [2] was our Lenten speaker for the evening, and I told him he had an hour and a half to do as he pleased. After speaking about love for a while he said that so often we talk about love and don't *do* it. We were going to *do* it. First we formed a huge circle around the hall. Then we turned, and while soft classical music played, massaged the back of the person to our left. Then after about ten minutes we did the same for the person on our right. After all that physical caring for one another he said we should go to five people, ask, "Will you let me love you?" and then express love any way we felt comfortable in doing. I could hardly believe our church, which has been experimenting with a number of experiences, and reaching out in search for more authenticity, would actually break through to the level of experience I saw happen. Two older men on our board of trustees came up and embraced one another. All over the hall people were laughing, smiling, hugging, expressing love and warmth.

As I tried to understand what had happened, it became apparent people had *received permission* to do what we so often only talk about. I can't discount the years of preparation that have gone on, the groups, the relational things we've done. Nor am I suggesting that was a moment of arrival. But it was beautiful, real, and illustrative. Dr. Osborne had shared with us many personal matters and lovingly led us into a time when, instead of being told to love each other, we felt secure in doing what many want to do and are not willing to risk. Obviously you don't go around asking people to love you, much less massaging fellow church members' backs. We hardly touch!

But we yearn for more touch, more assurance, more love,

and the good feeling that comes in sharing love. We do need to grow to a trust level where we *can* ask to have some of our needs met. Permission! Who is to give us permission? Who is to give someone else permission, thereby creating a mutually satisfactory experience? Me? You?

3

Can You Celebrate Yourself?

It has taken years for me to realize how deep my feelings of inferiority were, and the Christian faith didn't help for a long time. I went from trying to prove and justify myself when I was outside the faith to self-loathing in the faith. "Deny yourself!" "Take no thought of yourself!" "Die to yourself!" Only one more step was left! "Hate yourself!" A stream of deep self-loathing exists in our Protestant culture. Reactions to it are reflected in our literature of self-glorification and the demand to do as we please. But many, many people still do not like themselves! The cults of free expression, free love, the physical body personified, hardly equip people, especially our youngsters, to face either their inner or the outer world. As I think back, I have done a little sampling of most of it and found only estrangement, loneliness, and lostness.

We have tried to deal with it by sophistication. I have met so many brilliant, learned, well-read, socially aware, polished, proper people who were like brittle, one-way glass. Any strong breeze, any knock on the door, any vibrations and swinging song one speculates would shatter them! But I have also met crude, unkempt, and socially inept individuals. They don't seem any happier either.

To dream and dance, to sing and sigh, to laugh and linger, to play as people—doesn't it seem to be a missing dimension of life?

27

Sam Keen, in his delightful, helpful book, *To a Dancing God*,[1] observes, "In practice we are taught that dreams, day-dreams, and fantasy are means of escape from the real world of decision, fabrication, and action. The typical attitude toward fantasy is reflected in Tennessee Williams' play, *Night of the Iguana*, where T. Lawrence Shannon suggests that the solution to the human dilemma is to get rid of the fantastic and stick to the realistic. Dreaming is a clandestine activity. The suspicion is abroad that poetic, mythic, and religious languages (all forms of organized fantasy and imagination) are subtle ways of lying or garnishing bitter reality with sweet but illusory dreams." But as he goes on to point out, strangely enough, a society dedicated to scientific systems has as much trouble with the will and action of men as does fantasy.

I still remember a gathering of some friends who share leadership in a common movement. Instead of having opening devotions or a speech for a keynote (normal procedures for starting such meetings), we played games. We divided up in groups, picked childhood games and then actually played them. One group aggressively played kick-the-can right down the middle of the room. Another group played London-bridge; a third, hide-and-go-seek. I was surprised at the abandonment of mature spiritual leaders. Everyone ended up joining the London-bridge group. There is simplicity and childlikeness in all of us that lingers near the surface. It is not only in the nostalgia of memory. There seems to be a potential aliveness that still desires the spontaneity of life we had when we were kids and played just for the fun of it.

William Barclay points out, "In every decision of life we are doing something to ourselves; we are making ourselves a certain kind of person; we are building up steadily and inevitably a certain kind of self and character; we are making ourselves able to do certain things and quite unable to do others." [2] Eric Berne says this is our life script, basically formed quite early, but one which we can change.

Yet so few I talk to have any idea of their real identity. They look at me with a strange questioning wonder when I suggest we ought to be able to celebrate ourselves. Even our goals can dull or blind us, and we can lose the spontaneity of life.

Dr. Sam Keen recalls his own pilgrimage, finally settling on the goal of a Ph.D. and teaching. "Trusting in such promises I endured the desert of graduate education. I accepted exile from the present as the price of purchasing a future that would give dignity and density to my existence. I turned aside from the task of cultivating the native soil of my experience and became a share-cropper in intellectual fields of absentee owners. . . . Yet I was rude to Sam Keen. I ignored his boredom, I repressed his fantasies, I resented his impatience with intellectual games, I silenced the voice of his senses that called out for delight, I turned off the inner music that sets his ideas and his body dancing. . . ." [3]

Occasionally you hear of something which immediately presses you very deep introspectively. I'll never forget a friend telling me of an experience he had in the Midwest that did that for him—and for me. He was called back to the funeral of a friend. The friend's mother had asked close friends of her son to help her decide on one word which would describe her son, a word she would use as an epitaph on his tombstone. As the friend thought about it, it challenged him to think what one word *he* would want to have engraved for all time *on his own tombstone* to be the witness of his life!

What one word would you like to have as the epitaph of your life? What would it be now? I know what I would like to have for mine! It is *celebration!*

To have my life seen as a celebration, a celebration of living, of giving, of God and his gifts, love and friends, purpose and meaning, hope and eternity—ah! That is what I want!

In order to celebrate yourself you have to know and love yourself. So many people seem to live unhappily, confused, and at best, entertained. They work their way through taxes to death. To think that on the average someone in the United States commits suicide almost every twenty minutes! How many others have tried and failed, or have

thought about it seriously? It makes you listen to someone
like Theodore Dreiser.

> I find life to be not only a complete illusion or
> mirage . . . at best, whatever man does is some-
> thing that can only prolong the struggles and
> worries and, for the most part, futile dreams of
> those with whom he finds himself companioned.
> . . . In short, I catch no meaning from all I have
> seen and pass quite as I came, confused and dis-
> mayed.

How sad! How horribly, poignantly, assuredly sad! And
so many who also find their lives to have so little meaning
are less philosophical or verbal. They are just unhappy! But
some of you have known yourself, as I have, to be a marvelous miracle of God, wondrously made. Thank God you
don't have to pass through life confused and dismayed.
Celebrate!

In all the confusion and self-contempt, it is being able to
love yourself and celebrate your own existence. It is allowing life to be a party even though at times it is held in the
shadow of sadness.

Is there a deeper meaning why men miss personal significance to their own existence? I have felt the little child's
mixed-up verse echoes the confusion of some people I know,
and it might be true for you, too!

> Twinkle, twinkle, little star,
> How you wonder what I are!

I was shocked to hear a psychiatrist's answer to a question
of how much we know of the human mind. If you represent
the mind as a hundred-page book, what we know about it
could probably be represented with the first page!

This is probably the most analyzed, yet hung-up and little-
understood age of any in recent centuries. Yet we don't
seem to know what we are. There are lots of suggestions,
but they all seem to point to the problem rather than suggest a cure.

- The know-yourself fad, from sensitivity groups (of which some can be very helpful) to nudity to moral nihilism. . . .

- The flight from reality under the guise of either help or discovery, through booze, tranquilizers, and drugs. . . .

- The militant underprivileged, and the militant overprivileged, ready to claim and seize what in their minds are their rights, however much they violate or desecrate the rights of others. . . .

- The hung-up who declare themselves free, which so often means staying free from responsibility. . . .

- The established people with their cool hypocrisy so often justified by church affiliation for credentials. . . .

- And the technocrats who fail to see what we have created is now starting to create us.

In the face of such struggles to find a satisfactory life-style, Christianity in times past has not always been helpful. It has vacillated in emphasis from what one has called an inordinate self-regard to self-hatred, despising the world, flesh, and the devil.

It is my belief Jesus Christ came as one who not only had answers. He *was* the answer! Now Jesus was a realist. He made us face both our glory and our shame. He knew we could never find fulfillment through self-improvement programs or escapism. Man was alienated from God, separated from the source, reason, and ultimate fulfillment of life. This is what one editor recognized as basic to understanding our problem.

You can throw out the whole impossible rigma-role of an inherited bloodtaint called sin . . . and still see every man and every generation of men getting crossed up between themselves and within themselves, not inevitably but invariably . . . You can know perfectly well you ought to live

in love, and still you don't . . . You can concur
in the use of every social strategy and psychiatric
maneuver toward the improvement of man . . .
and still suspect the healthy-minded products need
forgiveness.[4]

Realist that Jesus was, he exposed our need to be changed
by holding up our possibilities. How about that! It's a good
deal different from the way we normally deal with the
inadequacies of others. Can you dare to believe you are forgiven, a miracle of God, the apple of his eye? If you can, you
can celebrate yourself, not forever despair of your sin.

Do you know why we don't love and care about our
neighbors? Because we don't love ourselves. How do we
change that? Well, loving ourselves begins when we know
ourselves as loved by God, forgiven and freed—really
knowing that experientially! That's where you start if you
want to learn how to celebrate yourself.

But first, *I believe one must understand what his or her
self-image is.* We all have that idea of what we are which
governs our thought and conduct, how we go about something, how we dress, our style of life. We accommodate that
self-image.

My eldest son and I were waiting in a shopping mall and
a teen-ager went by hunched over, dressed in a ridiculously
long, old army coat and very wide bell-bottoms. It was
something to watch him shuffling along with a funny
Groucho Marx gait.

It wasn't long before an attractive young girl came by
with her parents. Her shoulders were back and she had a
pleasant smile and good grooming. I suggested to Jeff that
each of those youths has his or her own image which dictates the way he or she dresses and walks. Now I am not
knocking young people, or the freedom to dress anyway one
wants to dress. Thank God for youth! Our youth have helped
to force us to rediscover sound, color, feeling, event, presence, process, spontaneity, and community. They have
helped us in a breakthrough in new dress codes and style,
and I am enjoying it! We have had such a sameness about
us. Most people live in the prison of the culture's image of

what they ought to look like. In fact, some live imprisoned in their own self-image, and they aren't free at all.

One woman I was counseling out of a severe depression was making progress, so I had a talk with her husband. He was a very fine fellow, deeply committed to Christ. But he was much too introverted and withdrawn for his wife. I suggested a new style for him. He said, "But I'm not that way." I told him, "You've not BEEN that way, but are you destined to always live with that old self-image? Be what God wants you to be today and tomorrow." He was God's man enough to respond to that challenge. What is your self-image? Are you free or imprisoned, unable to break out, discover God's love and forgiveness for you, love yourself and express it to others?

A second help for me that I find I must continually remind myself of is to *know what my divine possibilities are.*

It took me some time to realize this, but one of my friends taught me something one day. Bruce Larson is a great human. I have admired his gifts and his ability over the years. One day I said, "I thank God for you." He surprised me by replying, "I thank God for me too!" He told me how he had suffered through the identity crisis of self-discovery. Even with a master's degree in clinical psychology, he had to discover that though he would always have some shortcomings and human failures, if he surrendered to God— believing God loved him, knew him by name, forgave him, and invested eternity in him—he could walk as a free and whole person.

He had done that. He had come to see he did have talents and gifts of worth, all God-given. He had also committed these for God to use. And use them God did! He was enjoying being used, and his joy of living and sharing life with others is evident to everyone he meets. He is now literally touching thousands personally and many more through his books and tapes.

It is surprising how many people admit they either have never thought about having divine gifts, or hearing of it, feel they have none. What I mean by divine gifts is a bit more than the gifts of the Spirit Paul lists in 1 Corinthians

14. Some of the loveliest people who have blessed my life were individuals with no great talent. But by their positive attitude toward life, or their warm affirmations, or sensitivity to little concerns, or the thoughtful note or gift at the right time, they blessed my life. Those are God-blessed attributes, and for my money, divine.

Some can very easily feel God passed out gifts to a very special few but not to them, and they are mediocre and their life is lackluster. But he is wiser than that. He has invested specific abilities that fit your personality and circumstances and mine. There are gems to be mined, precious stones to be cut and polished, as Henry Drummond so aptly put it a century ago, acres of diamonds around us all, waiting to be discovered. Begin to believe it. See in your mind's eye a vision of yourself enjoying gifts you will begin to discover and use. Meditate on it, and allow your subconscious mind to reveal it to you.

See yourself as someone God specifically knows and loves, and has invested with great possibilities!

When I accepted Christ as Lord, I believed I became a Christian. Everything else should follow. But it didn't. I found that surrender to God is not a mere moment of truth and commitment. It is a way of life. So, a third necessary help has been to *recognize those things in myself that I continually do which are not under God's direction* and which keep me in the driver's seat, rather than Jesus Christ. *I have to turn them over to God, so I can begin to accept God's love.*

Many people I have counseled who had physical or emotional problems have been healed when they discovered the difference between running their own lives and letting Christ be Lord!

One fellow is rather typical and I will never forget him. He was a draftsman and, for a fellow of twenty-five, already sickly with a serious ulcer. He was a good man and attended church quite regularly. We got into a Bible study group together, and one night the conversation became very personal. It ended in his personal evaluation of his own understanding of commitment to Christ as his Lord. By faith he began to believe Christ was alive and in charge. He could trust him with his decisions and problems. That meant surrender and release! Within forty-eight hours his ulcer was healed, and he was off his milk and soft foods diet. It had such an effect that the marriage took a turn for the better and a previously childless couple soon had a baby on the way!

Interestingly, a year later we were talking and I asked him how his stomach was coming along. He said the ulcer had come back and was acting up. I said, almost flippantly, "Oh, taken your life back into your own hands, I see." He was shocked and admitted that, as a matter of fact, he guessed he had. A new resolve followed and weeks later the ulcer disappeared for good. So, deal with the roadblocks between you and Jesus Christ as master of your day by day living, and surrender. Living a surrendered life gives you freedom to celebrate yourself. Then you can *renew your hope, reclaim your value, revive your enthusiasm, and rededicate your abilities and gifts.*[5]

God has missed no one in investing usable, valuable gifts. What are yours? Is Christ using them?

If this is confusing to you, pray for insight for its particular meaning for your life. I have seen an arthritic patient, so crippled she could only move her head about ten degrees. But her ministry was her smile and a deep, prayerful interest in everyone who came to see her.

Some people have to face very difficult situations every day with physical limitations or job or health problems. But what I am talking about is not a self-help attitude to psychologically encourage them. Live believing you belong to the great God of the universe. You are under the lordship of Christ himself. Then his very resources will break open to you, and you will be able to celebrate yourself, even under adversity.

On the other hand, I have seen healthy, beautiful humans destroy their talented lives, dissipating their possibilities with alcohol, suicide, or just selfish apathy and personal pleasure.

Thank God for yourself, his gifts in you, his talents given you, his opportunities through you, the hope before you.

Someone pointed out that in the lectionary of devotional

guidelines I once prepared on this subject, I made a mistake and I wrote, "A few of us may have made noteworthy attainments in the world, but most of us are God's *nobodies*." I meant to write, ". . . most of us are God's somebodies." Whatever attainment or talent or feeling of a lack of it, you are God's somebody with worth and purpose. Discover what it is, and thank God for yourself. Love yourself and you will find how you can love others.

Life is a serious business. So much so, that I find sometimes a need to reaffirm the funny side, just for perspective. So I feel it is important to *see the humor in life and not be afraid to laugh at yourself*. I was recently having lunch with some clergymen, and one man kept saying how assured he was of God's calling. He admitted with great humility he was probably failing in many ways. But I sensed the humility was superficial and self-conscious, and that underneath was pride, defensiveness and little latitude or humor.

If he could have seen how funny he was in some ways and laughed at himself, he would have known he really IS God's man and doesn't need to protect or defend himself at all. He would have been less defensive and ridiculous, more open and warm, and much more able to enjoy the others of us who were trying to claim fellowship together. It is when my family laughs at me and I'm secure enough in their love to laugh with them that I get a new grip on life.

The other day in a meeting one thing after another went wrong. Everyone recognized it and that could have been a great opportunity for a sad-sack session. But we laughed and someone said, "Lord, this is a joke! We might as well relax and enjoy all these dumb faux pas that have happened." How the day lightened!

See the humor in life and have a good laugh now and then, even at yourself. You will be able to celebrate your security and freedom which need be in Christ alone.

But perspective is so important, isn't it? Unless we keep our concern to be free and whole in perspective, recognizing all we have and are is from God and accountable to him, it can become more self-concern. Paul could say, "I must boast

. . . may [no one] think more of me than he sees in me or hears from me" (2 Cor. 12:1–6). But he had sorted out his life in terms of God's will and surrendered all. He died daily to that surrender. Maybe that is why he was so confident. But some people never give a thought to responsibility of the use of their time, money, energies and the influence of helping or improving the lives of others.

What prevents you from knowing your true worth, from loving yourself properly and celebrating your life? Do you feel you are God's person without reservation? What keeps you from it? Is your life in your own hands or Christ's? Have you committed, actually dedicated, your gifts, talents, personality, whatever you have and are to him? What is your witness? If you were to die today, what one word would you like to have inscribed as your epitaph as a witness to future generations? How about seriously trying to answer those question for yourself? Just think.

Once we were no people. Now we are God's people. Once we lived in darkness. Now we walk as children of light. Once we had no purpose. Now we are ambassadors for Christ, God making his appeal through us, the appeal of an abundant life!

Love yourself as much as Christ loves you, and watch life take a new turn—as you begin to celebrate yourself.

> The joy of life is mine,
>   And cause I have to sing,
> God loves me here and now,
>   His hand's in everything.
>
> Life holds no terror then,
>   No victim of some fate.
> I love myself as God does,
>   And I can celebrate.

4

How Can We Celebrate, Feeling As We Do?

It was a revealing moment. This was a group where real feelings had come out—fears, frustrations, angers, desires. One young girl had a weepy attitude, obviously overwhelmed by the discussion, and finally she broke out into tears. The leaders weren't embarrassed as so often we are, falsely comforting in order to avoid participating in the deep traumas of another's life. They asked about the hurt inside which motivated the tears. The story she told was of a frightened little girl who now was a *grown-up* frightened little girl.

She was married and had had two miscarriages. Now she was carrying her third child. She so wanted to keep that baby and be a mother. What we saw happen in the time that followed was a beautiful thing. Slowly this young girl exposed the hurt and the fear inside her mind. As she gained confidence through the love, support, and acceptance of those around her in the group, she began to feel a new desire to be a mother. She came to understand that she was no longer under the bondage of fear. It had no hold on her. She was a woman with the marvelous prospect of motherhood ahead of her, a woman to be loved and to love.

In this group of understanding people she faced the negative and destructive feelings she had harbored. She graduated from that frightened little girl, who undoubtedly would have had another miscarriage, into a lovely young

lady whom I have heard delivered a beautiful child to love
and nourish into life. She had feelings buried within her
which could have destroyed her—feelings, I am sure, which
her conscience had inhibited her from expressing because
they were "wrong" feelings. When the dam broke, flushing
them out, new waters of life could flow.

We have been passing through a very interesting period
in our American culture. There is an emphasis presently on
feelings. I was a bit surprised to see the editorial page of
The Christian Century [1] magazine some time ago express a
conservative point of view on this trend. The editors sarcas-
tically said that these are good times for the body. Hardly a
day passes without someone giving the impression that redemption is coming through some new guru by way of celebrating some bodily experience. They pointed out the
obvious! Sensitivity training for executives, marathon
weekends for couples and singles, group therapy for the
healthy as well as the ill, all attempt to help people break
open the hidden dimensions of their lives and allow them
to be whole—as feeling creatures, some for the first time.
Some of that criticism might be justified. And we *have*
lived for too long in a sterile church atmosphere. Sure, some
probably have rejoiced and gone overboard in breaking out.
There has tended to be an attitude that suggested we should
not be emotional. Athletic events are the exception, but
generally we shun showing emotions. We hide our tears. It
is especially unmasculine to cry. Only the irrational get
angry, and it is usually only associated with the belligerent
and dissenting. I seldom lose my temper, but I remember
the day at the church that I did. Everyone was horrified!

Fear, anxiety, doubt, despair are usually lumped together
with anger as signs of weakness. So we tend to be inhibited
in telling anyone, hiding feelings even from our friends. Or
we repress them, forcing them from our consciousness and
covering these explosive feelings with, at best, temporary
containment. At times we are successful, and some play the
game nobly all their lives. But most emotions find some
outlet of expression, if not in verbalization or confession,
then in physical malfunctions. Could your ulcers, arthritis,

high blood pressure, depression, drinking patterns, and even paranoia be telling you something?

The behavioral sciences are publicly affirming owning our feelings, and it is almost like discovering a very old truth. It is okay to have feelings! It is normal to have negative emotions. It is even healthy to admit to them. But as much as we can understand that intellectually, it is still difficult sometimes to deal with the reality of what we do feel within. There is a significant difference between acknowledging the very human nature of certain feelings and placing a moral value of good or bad on them. It is okay to feel anger. It is natural and normal. How you handle it might be good or bad for you or others.

Of course in many churches there is a studied avoidance of emotion. Careful, quiet decorum has passed for sanctity.

I was thrilled to have an ancient myth destroyed at our former church. We were having a workshop on contemporary music in the large, old, staid Gothic sanctuary, and a pastor-choir master team specializing in new songs of celebration encouraged, of all things, an eight-year-old to RUN IN CHURCH and the congregation to laugh, clap, snap their fingers, and celebrate.

The church has had difficulty handling emotions. Negative and destructive feelings have been labelled wrong, just as being too happy has been suspect. Yet people have had these volatile feelings. So, people condemn either themselves or others when they occur. This has contributed to frustration and, in some cases, sickness. Furthermore, it has forced the church to become a game-playing institution where we must always try to lead from strength and cover up our weaknesses. You dare not laugh too loudly, or cry at all, lest you be labelled as unstable, and it gets out on the grapevine that you have a problem.

But Jesus was a feeling person. He wasn't ruled by his emotions, but he experienced them. He took them into account. He felt things deeply, and we sense how involved he became in the lives of those with whom he came in contact. Compassion for the adulterous woman about to be stoned to death—for the centurion whose servant was ill—the leper, a social outcast; anger for those who had made the church a mockery by profiting from worshippers with pigeon sales for their sacrifices; sorrow in the personal loss of his friend Lazarus, who had died while he was away; sorrow for a whole city of countrymen who had missed the day of their visitation, their opportunity to respond to God's will. Jesus weeping over a city! Here is a God who understands our feelings because he made us, created us in his own image, made us to be feeling people because he is a feeling God.

When our church showed the movie *The Gospel According to St. Matthew* a few years ago, it was most interesting to see the emotions and concerns it raised in the people attending. How much more easily we have accepted portrayals of a Jesus meek and mild, gently cooing the Sermon on the Mount. But here was an angry, almost hostile young man. It pressed a number of people to at least reconsider the story and their personal images of the Lord in their imaginations. The value, obviously, of the movie was not whether it was an accurate interpretation of how Jesus looked and acted, but the inner dialogue it created in each of us as viewers. It also said something about our own feelings and emotions in connection with what we believed and thought and about how we dealt with those feelings. For the issue of celebrating this marvelous life God has given us to share with others is not the rightness and wrongness of our feelings. It is dealing with the reality of them.

Someone has remarked, "The face that you have when you are twenty is no fault of your own, but the face you have when you are fifty is your own, and you deserve it."

We are responsible. Wonderfully made, I am increasingly aware of how we corrupt the system and bring on much of our own ill health, many of our interpersonal problems, much of our vocational unhappiness and general dissatisfaction with life. What can we do about it? There could be many more, but I see at least these suggestions in the Bible.

First: *We can face our feelings honestly.*

The Bible says, "But take heed to yourselves lest your hearts be weighed down" (Luke 22:34). A great deal is said in the church about wrong feelings, hate, resentment, lust, and selfishness. Anyone sensitive and listening can develop a tremendous guilt. We all have these feelings of hate and love, lust and longing, despair and pettiness, childishness and rascality at one time or another. Some people have some of these feelings more often than others. But they are there in all of us. The first step toward redeeming our emotional life and being in charge is to honestly face whatever we are really feeling, to own our feelings.

Second: *We need to get to the root of our feelings, to know their causes and origins.*

I would never minimize the difficulty of understanding ourselves completely! But I know there is a reason behind every feeling, and I am ever amazed at what I continue to discover about myself when I look for that reason.

The easiest way is to always blame others for our problems and project on them our hostilities, frustrations, and anxieties. Sometimes it isn't that we need to be improved upon so much as it is that we need to have some understanding of what we are wrestling with on the interior of our beings. This is what can corrupt, distort, and misuse the stuff of life. John Henry Newman might have been right, "Man is not a creature that needs to be improved, but a rebel that needs to lay down his arms . . ."

When we stop defending ourselves, daring to believe we can be completely secure in Jesus Christ, we won't have to try to improve. We can stop the rebel will that fends off God and defends the self against others. It will simply amaze you the insight you'll receive as to the source and reason for many feelings that have been troubling you and how they no longer have power over you.

Let the Master master your mind, and you will understand what Jesus meant. He urged us to get to the real reasons for our feelings, especially in our interpersonal relationships.

> Why do you see the speck that is in your brother's eye, but do not notice the log that is in your own eye? . . . first take the log out of your own eye, and then you will see clearly to take the speck out of your brother's eye (Matt. 7:3, 5).

Third: *We can deal with our feelings, especially if we believe they do not satisfy what could be best for us.*

The Bible says this in connection with misuse of the sacrament of Communion. But it is also applicable on a much broader scale—"That is why many of you are weak and ill, and some have died. But if we judged ourselves truly, we should not be judged . . ." (1 Cor. 11:30–31). If there are feelings which we judge are wrong coursing through us, we must deal with them creatively. We need an outlet. One friend told me of tremendous anxiety and resentment over a conflict with a colleague. He went up in the mountains on a lonely hill and screamed himself free! He is not a neurotic, but one of the most stable, clear, free Christians I know, alert to mental health, and free to be honest and do something about his feelings. But acting as if we do not feel a certain way or repressing it is a step toward illness, not freedom.

Complaining is not the answer either, any more than self-pity is. Dr. Hobart Mowrer, former research professor of psychology at the University of Illinois and a past president of the American Psychological Association, writes, "It has been my consistent observation that if, instead of complaining, one tries *confessing*, others do not get impatient, and genuinely useful things start happening."

Dr. Mowrer continues, "When we stop talking about how much we hurt and get down to the (good and sufficient) *reasons* for our discomfort, the effect is dramatically different. The Bible says, 'Confess your sins' (and also your feelings which are bothering you?) 'to one another, and pray for one another, that you may be healed' " (James 5:16).

Talking it out with an understanding friend is important for mental health and for spiritual wholeness. In fact, I am almost ready to be dogmatic and say that we ought to talk about our feelings with someone else before we talk about them to God. We can be very vague—and generous—with ourselves when we talk to God. But it seems when we have to be honest with a friend about how and why we feel as we do, we get down to facts. One way of dealing with our feelings is to build a new base for them. If your feelings trouble you, if your emotional outlook needs improving—especially if you recognize that your outlook on life is poor and far less than God meant for you—you might need to reprogram your attitude toward life.

How many people do you know who have the outlook of Arthur Rubinstein?

> I'm passionately involved in life: I love its changes, its colors, its movement. To be alive, to be able to see, to walk, to have houses, music, paintings . . . it's all a miracle. I have adopted the technique of living life from miracle to miracle . . . what people get out of me is this outlook on life which comes out in my music.

That so excites me! I want to be that kind of person, and so do you! We might not have the musician's skill, but we have many ordinary human contacts every day. In the circumstances of our present position does a gratitude and joy emote from our lives?

When we believe Jesus Christ has control of our mind, and he is charging every experience with his presence, our feelings can change! If we dare to throw all of our convictions into believing that, we will discover how life can become living from miracle to miracle! Why not? Doesn't the Bible encourage us? "Be transformed by the renewal of your mind, that you may prove what is the will of God, what is good and acceptable and perfect" (Rom. 12:2). Let Christ be the base for a new attitude toward life, and he will master your mind and emotions in a new joy of living.

A fourth way to deal with our feelings creatively: *Use common sense.*

We waste time and energy fighting situations we can't change. Maybe in part, this is what the Bible means when it encourages us, "Those who have believed in God may be careful to apply themselves to good deeds; these are excellent and profitable to men. But avoid stupid controversies . . . " (Titus 3:8–9). The Prayer of Serenity alcoholics use should be second to the Lord's Prayer for us,

"God grant me the serenity to accept the things I cannot change, courage to change the things I can, and wisdom to know the difference."

A fifth thought. It is my observation that few people have learned to enjoy the beautiful people around them as God counts them beautiful and loves them. This can begin by *broadening our emotional base to embrace the feelings of others*. The Bible encourages us, "Rejoice with those who rejoice, weep with those who weep. Live in harmony . . ." (Rom. 12:15–16). We live in a world of trauma and hurt and need, of great issues to be addressed, of masses of people to be understood and loved—all sometimes summed up in individuals who live on the edges of our lives. We will not be smothered in our own self concerns when we begin to embrace the feeling world of others.

To use C.S. Lewis's phrase, you will be "surprised by joy" to discover how often God has preceded you there. Common, ordinary people under such attention are like common beach stones, wet by your kindness, shining—polished by your concern and love, absolutely beautiful! Take a chance on dipping into the emotional stuff of their lives, as an adventurous risk. In fact, this is one way I believe we glorify God.

One last, significant factor:

However you want to call it, whatever method you want to use, we can *tune in to the divine*. Henry Drummond said, "Ten minutes spent in Christ's society every day, aye, two minutes, if it be face to face, and heart to heart, will make the whole life different." Yokefellows suggest that a half hour each morning in quiet meditation, Bible reading, and prayer will bring significant results. The Bible urges us to ". . . walk by the Spirit" (Gal. 5:25). Tuned in to him, for he's as close as breathing! Your emotions can be attuned with the joy of being and doing. You were made to be a feeling person.

How about it? Do your emotions help you celebrate life? Face your feelings. What dominates your desires dominates you. Dare to believe Jesus Christ is taking them and handling them, and your whole being will be a celebration.

The Spirit's life
　　to be my law,
O God, to set me free . . .

Though even bruised,
　　Lord, to be used,
O Master, master me.

5

*Celebrate Your Sexuality**

Try an experiment. Out of the blue, just say *sex* in the middle of a conversation with people. See the reaction! Do it with a church group, and the reaction will be even more noticeable. For we have a tremendous hang-up on the whole area of sex and really do not know what to do about it. We live in what *Life* magazine called "the era of sexuality." [1]

Sex is a very popular subject among Christian writers today, much less the pulp and slick magazine and paperback writers by the thousands. You can find a horde of material addressing the subject, "A Christian View of Sex." But as Christians, we still do not know how to handle—not just the subject—but the very sexual dynamic of our own personalities. When I spoke on the subject some time ago, using some of the material in this chapter, it was interesting to note the negative and rather censorious reactions I received. For it was "out of place" and "not in good taste." Just the title of this chapter might make some apprehensive. Preconceptions are feeding your computer right now, ready to prejudice and filter the material ahead of you here. It just proves the cultural problem created for us on this natural, wonderful, confusing, exciting, and disturbing dimension of our human personality.

* Maybe this chapter ought to be entitled "Celebrating Our Sensuality," allowing our sexual nature to be considered in its rightful role as only a part of a broader understanding of the beauty of our senses.

Since I was quite small I naturally thought this dimension was a marvelous part of being me. I was fascinated with the child games such as "doctor-nurse" we invented in the neighborhood when parents weren't around. I didn't know that discovering the difference between myself and the little girls down the block was "dirty." It didn't take long! It was soon communicated in a very clear, negative way.

So, to admit even now that the opposite sex pleases me risks suspicion. Many perversely read into this with a mind-set which through the years has implied that sexual attraction is "sick" and certainly *not* to be celebrated.

In defense then, let me say I am happily married to a very attractive woman who "turns me on." We have four children, two of whom are pretty daughters, growing into lovely womanhood. While my marital status places me in a personal context of responsibility with boundaries and limitations, it does not limit my general feelings for the opposite sex. Most women do not approximate the exceptional specimens in the centerfolds of men's magazines, but they are still attractive. For each of us has our own attributes and attractive traits. Eric Berne, in his fine book *What Do You Say After You Say Hello?* captures it. "Anatomy makes one photogenic," but beauty comes from within, and is in the appreciation we have for a person.

You might think we don't need more, but less consideration of an overworked subject. Hardly a popular magazine does not have something to offer on sex. But if in this book we are to talk about life as a celebration, we have to seriously consider our sexuality. This is a vital part of being a person. Furthermore, as I have pointed out already, there is mounting evidence of tremendous confusion, of subliminal protest in our youth, confusion with well-meaning adults, and unmet needs in many people. When I was gathering data a couple years ago, the statistics read three thousand new cases of venereal disease reported every day in the United States and more than one million illegal abortions performed every year. Three hundred thousand illegitimate births were recorded each year, though fourteen states kept no records of illegitimacy. One out of sixteen girls will probably become pregnant out of wedlock before reaching twenty years of age, and this represents a cross-section of American social and economic structure.

How far this is from the beautiful celebration of life as God made us to experience it! The joy of our sexuality does not come from fear, legislation, condemnation, and inhibition. But it will not be discovered and preserved without understanding the context of dignity, purpose, responsibility, and character.

So, while I might not contribute greatly to the mass of academic literature on the subject, I hope sharing my personal observations will give some perspective and encouragement to many confused people. I don't believe we should leave it to the hedonists! I don't believe nice people don't talk about it (though, as you have noticed, many "nice and proper" people still make naughty little jokes with strong sexual overtones to their humor, soliciting nervous laughter). I don't think Christians should just deny, condemn, rationalize, or hide the subject. There is something great and wonderful about our sexuality that is part of celebrating life that we can claim. Let's try once more for a sane understanding.

It was amusing to read of even Michael Murphy of Esalen Institute's sensitivity laboratory in California giving this testimony, "Well, it finally happened. A young person came up to talk with me and I couldn't tell if this person was a man or a woman. Now I've seen plenty of young people of both sexes, dressed in slacks, sweaters and long hair, but I have always been able to find *some* sexually distinguishable clue. *This time there was no way for me to tell.* I admit it shook me up. I didn't know exactly how to relate. I felt it would take a new kind of relating, no matter if it were a boy or girl." [2]

Dr. Cyrus Pangborn of Rutgers University has an interesting counter-thought about the new dress of youth, long hair and look-alike clothes which bears directly on this subject. He believes that hair and clothing styles do not have that much to do with sex, that they are externals, and that true sexuality is not inhibited or changed by these things. He says that the look-alike dressing of boys and girls might be an unconscious protest against the idea so many have that sex is external, that they might be indirectly claiming inner awareness of sexuality to be recovered only when the externals are deemphasized.[3]

We do need to reclaim an inner awareness of real sexuality and what it means for us as humans and as God's children. For sex is part of a moral crisis of our times.

Marshall McLuhan and George Leonard stated in an article that sex as we know it may soon be dead, because sexual concepts, practices, and ideals are being altered almost beyond recognition. I doubt it. But it's a sobering observation.

Distortion is everywhere. I thoroughly enjoy a little foreign car I drive. I believe it is well-engineered, and maybe it's because I appreciate certain mechanical features of it that I considered and then purchased it. But I remember my first real attention was drawn to the name in an ad in a good glossy magazine. A picture of the car was featured with a shapely brunette draped over the fender. It had nothing to say about its superior engineering, roadability, or enjoyment. There was only an innuendo double-playing some statement about "the second most appreciated Italian body." The superficial externals of so-called "sex" have been used and misused in advertising in almost every field.

However, if you give any real examination to this situation, you see that true sexuality has not been glorified or celebrated. It's been confused and missed. Usually only the exterior of the *female* body has been given attention and called "sex," suggesting the ultimate of sexuality is intercourse, with attention only on the woman. It has usually been eroticism or biology and not sexuality which has been considered.

J.B. Priestley, the famed British author of some nineteen novels and twenty-four plays, sees eroticism as possibly an expression of hatred of woman and a fear of true love and sex, but obviously an exploitation of the profit motif and one of the worst features of Western civilization. He points out that even in the best of books there is that suggestion of sadistic eroticism, and at lower levels a deliberate pandering of our worst feelings. And sad to say, we cannot either discount or disprove him.

We, the customers, are supposedly more free today about the sexual side of man than ever before. Absolutely nothing is withheld from public display. Yet we are as confused, inhibited, and preoccupied with the sexual as any before us. Living in declared freedom, we are bound up so much so that our kids, whom we self-righteously condemn as being immoral and loose, are saying, "Our parents' generation is hung-up about sex."

They are right! It is not the youth but the adults who pander the erotic and profit from it. It is adults who distort the meaning of sex by fighting adequate information through public schools while failing their responsibilities in the homes. A chaplain of one of our technological schools is jabbing us where it hurts—"The prudential sex ethic, based on nothing but fear, made moral morons of us all; now we can make decisions about sexual behaviour on the basis of a positive understanding of sexuality. . . . The family, which traditionally exacted an often tyrannous self-conformity in exchange for the security it provides the child, is now in a position to become a supportive setting in which the young have the freedom to explore value systems other than those of their parents. . . ."

Yet the truth is that few seem to know where to find a value system worth basing their lives on, a value system with a power at the heart of it that is stronger than the glands. Consequently emotional wreckage is everywhere. It is most profoundly seen in unstable home life. One out of every four marriages ends in divorce (one out of three if the partners are teenagers), and someone has estimated that one out of the other three marriages still holding together is floundering in unhappiness.

If you really think about it, you will see those who supposedly glory in sex really do not. They glory in the erotic, which is the sexual out of context. They usually pervert and distort. This comes from a crisis of relationship. There are a number of accompanying personality problems—insecurity, loneliness, unfulfilled relationships, and identity crises. People often use sex as an escape or a comfort for other psychological needs.

The urbanization of man has not helped. It has often helped destroy what semblance of the personal people had. Few have the old family homestead and the stability, identity, continuity, and respect of their heritage. Modern man has been zip-coded and punch-carded and organized, housed and dressed in production-line sameness. Powerless and impersonal, men and women find one of the most intimate expressions of their personhood in their sexuality as a means of reclaiming meaning and love.

What happens, however, is that they end up in further confusion. When we take a gift of God which is natural and try to make it a means to an end, it often ends a vice. J.B. Priestley is helpful again, clarifying this matter of eroticism. He sees it as the desire for a sensation and not a person, therefore excluding love. There is even the danger that too much eroticism will eventually prevent a person from being able to experience true sexual love. But this kind of love isn't easy as thousands of trashy writings suggest. The more people become insecure, bewildered, and fearful, the more there has been an increased emphasis in fiction, movies, and advertising "upon the value and joy, the magical saving grace, of sexual love. This is not necessarily wrong, but it can be argued that we now are asking sexual love to shoulder too many burdens in a fairy-tale atmosphere in which everybody can 'live happily ever after.' "

So, sexuality is perverted into eroticism! It is a crisis of personhood and relationship! We use sex to answer deeper needs and, twisting what is to be beautiful and normal, fail both to discover personhood or to enjoy our sexuality.

It has to be admitted that the church has not always been most helpful either. An old chestnut is that Presbyterians do not know how to take away sin. They just keep you from enjoying it. It might be stretched to say that the church has not always known what to do with sex, the sexual nature of man, always throbbing to find expression. Unable to eliminate it, it has just kept us from enjoying it!

The Apostle Paul might have had his own problems. But what is recorded as his writing in a time thought to be the end of the age, suggests it is better (a second best) to marry than burn! Now really!

Historically, the early church had to work out a view of sex to meet the obvious importance of this ingredient of man's life. They faced both tremendous immorality in the culture and the fact that the end of the world just did not come to finish it all. Rather than accept the Gnostic view that the flesh was evil, the early apologists acknowledged the wholeness of man, sexual as well as spiritual. But in order to organize and control the dynamic problem (and our sexual nature is so often problematic!), this was their rationale. Man's sexual activity was illicit. Celibacy came to be glorified by a celibate clergy, with a virgin mother of Jesus held up as the epitome of womanhood.

Life in the flesh was morally acceptable so long as it was aimed at procreation and procreation was controlled within the bonds of marriage. Times have changed but the problem hasn't. First-century answers do not meet twentieth-century issues. Today we still need help in understanding our sexuality. If we are to believe most responsible demographers (those who plot population trends), there is still danger that we are going to crowd and starve ourselves off this planet with uncontrolled procreation. Unmarried people also have a legitimate question when they ask if true sexuality of man is to be defined only in terms of procreation and reproduction. Married people have demanded new attitudes toward contraception. We are legitimately seeking new understanding of moral responsibility regarding abortion in the face of human dignity, over-population, and sanctity of life.

But is the answer more information? I do not believe it is. A professor of religion at one college says that whatever is wrong with sex in our culture today, it is certainly not because we do not get enough information! He suggests it might be because we have taken it too seriously. We might be as wrong in emphasizing sex as something we must get total joy out of as a result of techniques and freedom from moral restraints as we were when we emphasized sex only for the utilitarian purpose of producing babies.

He further observes that today it is work, not play. Even *Playboy* insinuates this attitude and not the freedom it proclaims, "A playboy must apply the right techniques, must cultivate the art of being a great lover, he is not free just to relax. . . ." But this professor's attitude of play runs the risk of making sex recreational—still something we *do*.

In the same way, I'm afraid the confusion will be increased, not dissipated, by the nomenclature "sex education." While I am in favor of sex education in the schools and churches, the impression is given that sex is primarily biological and glandular. We proudly brag about how matter-of-fact we have been in presenting the "facts of life" unemotionally. This can be as misleading as the other extreme of the glossy, romantic image or sick eroticism all under the title "sex."

The truth is that true sexuality is not to be defined in terms of procreation which is task-oriented, producing children, nor recreation which is self-centered, using another for personal pleasure. Both might well exist or result. But *true sexuality is relational with one's Creator and his intention and will, with one's self, one's manliness or femininity, and with others in appreciation of the manliness or femininity of others as persons.* Healthy sexuality will recognize it as God's creation and people as dynamic persons to be loved and respected.

No matter how old we are or in what state we find ourselves—married, single, widowed—we should appreciate sexuality as a considerable force in life. It is to be *re*creative whereby we are renewed as God's person, enjoying ourselves and others.

At a conference an older woman whom I had met only once was casually walking ahead of me to a meeting. Her dress was unzipped in back. I joked about her not being put together and offered to zip her up. Then, as we walked

along, without thinking I impulsively gave her a hug. I
sensed it would be all right, and it was. She later told me
she enjoyed that hug. She had no apparent sexual problems,
was not looking for an affair, nor was I. It was spontaneous
and enjoyable. She was affirmed as a woman and, though
happily married, felt this was a nice gesture which she
could enjoy.

Why make such a big issue of such a simple thing? Because many people would suggest that I was "working
something out," that I had some "need," or that I had over-
stepped "propriety." I can't help but feel the problem is
in them regarding a lack of freedom in the feeling-touch
area of interpersonal relationships. It reflects one of the
inhibiting dimensions of our culture. But worse, it is part
of a process which has inhibited the normal, what I would
call "general sexual nature" of us all. It forces us to consider
these gestures, expressions and feelings as tainted, suspicious and finally to be intensified in bizarre and "loaded"
attitudes. Some intuitively feel this. But they project their
feelings, insinuating suspicious motivations for those who
act more freely than they do. Looking back on such a trivial
but typical situation as I mentioned above, it *did* have sexual overtones, but they were normal, enjoyable and harm-
less.

Incidentally, we later had a deep conversation. This was
a woman of fine education who was a denominational executive and had travelled the world. She was seminary-trained
and well read. In the course of a very enlightening conversation, I commented that most men suffer in silence over
their lusts. They think they must be "oversexed" because of
how easily attracted they are to women and how often they
fantasize about sex. They joke about it as sort of a confession therapy. Her comment was that this is in no way an
exclusive male problem, for women feel the same way. I
countered by suggesting that men and women feel differently, really approaching sex from opposite viewpoints. I
was surprised to hear her deny that. She observed that
this was what we do on most subjects. We put women in a
different frame of reference, and the written material about

it is authored by men. We still have much to learn about such a natural implicit part of our nature which we share!

Now this might surprise you, but I don't believe the "sensual" is evil either! It wasn't meant to be. "Frequently we consider those things sinful which someone else enjoys." [4] By definition it has become so, "a preoccupation with gratification of carnal appetites, lacking in moral restraints, lewd, unchaste." So you have a book like *The Sensuous Woman*. Even though it contains some helpful, honest insights about a woman's approach to sexual relationships with a mate, it still comes off with a testimony to immorality, self-centered gratification and perversion, and destroys again the potential understanding for Christians of legitimate sexuality. As a derivative of the word *sense* or feeling, *sensual* is obviously a neutral word. It is the context, the moral system in which we understand it, which gives it meaning and the potential absence or presence of enjoyment.

Father Rivers says, "A friend of mine used to accuse me of being sensual—which of course I always admitted and even defended. . . . I argued that being sensual was part of being human and I simply had no chance at being anything else (certainly not angelic). Well, he based his conclusion about my sensuality (the word to be taken pejoratively, of course, and inflected in such a way as to connote abhorrence and disgust) on the fact that I liked bright colors . . . seasoning . . . warm weather. . . ." [5]

The issue is that many people have not had a life based on a value system with power and joy at the heart of it. The test of that value system is if it gives control, respect, love and fulfillment to our humanity. Does it celebrate our senses as God intended? Does it make life significant, responsible, and worthwhile as well as enjoyable as long as we live?

Jesus said the issue is not what you do but what you are. Someone has wisecracked that you are getting old when the gleam in your eye is from the sun hitting your bifocals. Looking lustfully at another, coveting your neighbor's husband or wife, does not create evil from the input! The evil comes from what is already within you. Our Lord said the problems that get us into trouble are not from what goes into us. He undoubtedly was talking about what we see and think as well as what we eat and drink.

"What comes out of a man is what defiles a man. . . . For from within, out of the heart of man, come evil thoughts, fornication . . . adultery, coveting, wickedness, deceit . . . foolishness . . ." (Mark 7:20ff).

"So if your eye is sound, your whole body will be full of light; but if your eye is not sound, your whole body will be full of darkness. If then the light in you is darkness, how great is the darkness!" (Matt. 6:22–23). We need a power at the heart of our value system that is stronger than our glands, which filters what we see and regulates what we think, and results in responsible actions and reactions. We need to affirm the sights and sounds and tastes and feelings of life. I wonder how many people have lost the wonder of the common good feelings of life! The other day I realized I had been so busy, rushing to meet deadlines, I wasn't enjoying much of anything. I came home late that night, and it was clear and beautiful outside. A full moon and stars were brilliantly shining in the sky; I took a deep breath of the sharp night air and asked myself how much of life I was feeling, sensing. How easy it is to lose touch with the common, good feelings of life.

The key is what we are because of *whose* we are. "If the eye is sound. . . ." This is not to close our eyes to that which is sexually stimulating or to deny what our senses indicate is enjoyable. It is to be full of light. Jesus said, "I am the light of the world."

I don't want to sound preacherish, but listen to the Answer. It says it so well. "This is the message we have heard from him and proclaim to you, that God is light and in him is no darkness at all. . . . If we say we have fellowship with him while we walk in darkness, we lie and do not live according to truth; but if we walk in the light, as he is in the light, we have fellowship with one another, and the blood of Jesus his Son cleanses us from all sin . . . " (1 John 1:5–7). "In him was life, and the life was the light of men" (John 1:4).

The inner presence of Jesus meets my need and the need of so many I've met who are not too different from me in their desire to be a whole person, enjoying their senses and their sexuality. When you know he is present, it gives you the security of being loved by God and having worth and purpose. You know you are filled with his life and light. He makes your eye sound, your mind and desires responsible, your attitude pure.

His presence within allows you to celebrate your sexuality, changing greed to gratitude, lust to love, sensuality to sensitivity, anxiety to appreciation, darkness to light.

It's great to be able to appreciate one's manliness or femininity, the sexuality of one another and ourselves within the fellowship of a new humanity because we walk in the Spirit as temples of the living God.

A teacher was surprised to have a little first grade girl burst into her room to breathlessly report that the first grade boys were catching the girls at the front entrance as they came out and kissing them. The teacher asked her why she did not use the side entrance. "Oh, no," the little girl replied. "Then they would miss me!" We all have our needs and we do not want to be missed in being appreciated or cared about and affirmed. But we are also susceptible to forgetting whose we are and letting our needs dictate our actions and our glands become our gods.

I chatted with a pastor at a conference a few years ago, and as I listened and appreciated him as a person, he opened his life more and more. Finally, he admitted desperation in his life, unhappiness in his ministry, because of an unfaithful relationship with another woman. She was fulfilling his deeper ego needs. He trusted me enough to confess it and released the relationship. After admitting his own need, he reclaimed Christ as his inner light and reaffirmed himself as a sexually needy but now freed person filled with God's love to be responsible to his wife.

I saw him a year later at the other end of the country and, with happiness written all over him, he told me of a marriage renewed, his personal life recharged and responsible, and his church refired!

Let's not be conformed to this world. Nor should we be intimidated! How we might be released to a new freedom to examine and validate our own humanity if we could each know the God of our creation affirming our basic nature! Why, we would be transformed! We should be!

Be honest for a moment. What are your psychological needs? How does being a man or a woman fit into it? Where do you feel there is sexual attractiveness in yourself? Where is there something unfulfilled? Can you admit those needs and affirm your sexuality as God-given? If you are married and still experience those outside attractions, honestly examine them. Sort out the frustration and lack of fulfillment from the natural sensual nature that affirms and enjoys the opposite sex in normal relationships. See how you can affirm it! Consider Christ's spirit alive in you, celebrating the created beauty, attractiveness, and spark in others. Know your weaknesses, limitations, responsibilities, and needs. Trust it all to a God who will keep you free, not only from sin, but for life and deeper relationships with others.

If you are single, claim the worth and significance of your whole person, including your sexuality. Recognize the limitations of the one side of the sexual drive, toward intercourse. But also see the other legitimate and enjoyable factor of being a sexual person; that is, enjoying and being enjoyed as a full and whole person in your masculinity or femininity. The touch, the embrace, Christian love, affirmation, all can have sensual dimensions (in the best *sense*) without being erotic or directional in the human family when plumbed by the radical love of Jesus Christ. He came, preventing us from ever using people for our own purposes, but loving and affirming all men as the beautiful creatures we each were meant to be.

You can celebrate your own sexuality and that of others. . . . "If your eye is sound . . . (for) your whole body will be full of light."

6

Rejoicing in Your Brother

I want to share a news article I clipped years ago from an editorial page under the title, "No Comment Department." The reason for the editors not commenting is apparent. It was regarding the founding of a new church in one of Chicago's suburbs.

While the new church was called, "The Church of Christian Liberty," one feels it could have been called, "The Church of the Elder Brother." The founder of the church is quoted in the *Chicago Daily News* as saying that the United States should have bombed, among other things, Wonsan Harbor in North Korea in retaliation for the loss of the EC–121 spy plane. The pastor's attitude toward foreign policy in the light of Jesus' teachings is interesting:

> I accept Jesus' statement that we should love our enemies. But there are negative manifestations of love as well as positive manifestations. Just like a parent spanks a child, we need to teach the North Koreans a lesson. They must be slapped—and slapped hard.

I am sure that the church he founded will grow. There are many people who would like to reclaim an image of retribution in the God whom they believe is on their side, whether it be in politics, foreign policy, or religion. They are terribly disturbed at the turn of events in our society which allows a voice to dissenters, acknowledges social cripples, practices tolerance for non-conformists, and seeks to understand, undergird, and encourage the misfits and the losers.

In a school paper to parents in a former town where we lived someone said as much,

> I've about reached the end of my tolerance for our society's one-sided sympathy for the misfit, the ne'er-do-well, the drug addict, the chronic criminal, the loser-in general, the Underdog. I feel it is time for someone to stand up and say, "I'm for the UPPERDOG!"

Obviously he believes he and his are UPPERDOGS and, therefore, champions his own. If he were a "loser," he would hardly have assumed such a self-righteous attitude.

The familiar story of the Prodigal Son has been generally renamed "The Parable of the Elder Brother." Stop a moment and read it (Luke 15:11–32). It is a classic example of our relationships with others and with God. It has given me a great deal of insight into my own life.

The elder brother had reached the end of *his* tolerance also. His father's one-sided sympathy for his misfit brother infuriated him. They had lost half of their family assets. *He* had lost part of it, because now with his brother back home, the ne'er-do-well would be living off *his* share of the property. He also would be living it up like a prince! Rings on his fingers, a new robe on his shoulders, and the fatted calf ready for market at a goodly price, slaughtered just for his homecoming party.

He'd never had a party thrown for him, and he was the one who kept things running smoothly, never complaining, always doing what was asked of him, day in, day out, doing his share and more. Sometimes *he* had wanted to take off, too! But he hadn't! The misfit, the loser got the attention—and the party!

It is obvious that Jesus was proposing a radical stance for our attitude toward others. I have often attributed the Protestant individualistic work ethic to our American heritage. A man's frontier faith in God and himself! I was raised to believe anyone can succeed if he has gumption and get-up-and-go. If you don't succeed, such logic dictates, then it is because you haven't had the willingness.

Such a myth has been developed by one of two kinds of people—those who have never been trapped by their environment, psychological makeup, or circumstances, or those who were, but luckily made it out. So often those who do break out of the prisons of economic and social depression soon forget how it was when they were helpless. Pride catches up with them, and they become as judgmental of their former state as those who have never shared it. They end up looking down on those who are now where they were. They are now "Upperdogs." The Master knew. He understood. The church he proposed would not be one built on the liberty of license, misusing our freedom to slap down those who continued to violate our rights. Nor would the fellowship he initiated be proud, looking down on the losers and the lost in contempt. However, such attitudes are natural for unredeemed man.

The Lord held out to man a new nature—loving the loser and wanting to share with him, having faith in those who broke faith, enabling them to see hope beyond their own capacity. This new man would create a place for the misfit because we are all misfits, save in our equality in the forgiveness and grace of God. So many are concerned with conformity that they miss the issue of individuality. But the issue of individuality is not "Can I do as I please?" for which the young son of the parable had originally asked and which the older son grudgingly realized he had never had the nerve or verve to seek. The issue is "What am I *to be* that will be pleasing—pleasing to the God who made me, to my neighbor who becomes an individual in relationship to other individuals like myself in community, to myself with whom I must live continually?"

Everyone is an expert on the problems of our day so long as they can cast judgments on others, blaming them. Some say that drugs are still the foremost social problem facing America. Those still fighting for social justice would say racism is still the number one problem; others say pollution and impending ecological disaster. And each has his own narrow answers, usually exclusive of other concerns. But the greatest preventative is a serious review of the deeper problem within each of us. It is a problem which turns many a marvelous, dynamic, inquiring young mind to dangerous experimentation in potential self-destruction, reacting to a world he did not make.

We are alienated like the elder son from the Father who made us. That alienates us from our fellowman with whom we hardly live, like the prodigal younger brother. And we will continue to be helpless if we think it is someone else's problem to be solved with new laws, greater education, more sophisticated controls, latitude in responsibility, greater technology and condemnation of the losers and the under-dogs.

The prodigal younger son might represent that portion of our society alienated and estranged. The elder son might represent all of us "proper" people. We feel we have so many rights because we have gone to work, done our job and conformed, and by and large stayed out of overt trouble. You *might* draw at least an insinuation from the parable then, that Jesus is suggesting that the burden of proof is not upon the younger son, but upon the elder one. The question is, *What are we inside* that communicates wholeness or lack of it? Where do we show judgment or a lack of condemnation and self-interest? Where is there desire to protect our own status quo or an honest desire to contribute to a situation, whether it is in our own homes, in our own community, or in our nation? What can we discover within ourselves which will most easily help all of us discover our personhood, potential, and purpose?

A German theologian is reported as observing that the problem today is not how to find a gracious God but how to find a gracious neighbor. We will become a gracious neighbor when we awaken to just how gracious God has been to us. When the elder son could get over his selfish concerns, forget the fact he had never had a party, and realize how gracious his father had been to him providing for all his needs—overlooking his failures and shortcomings and forgiving him for his own less-dramatic infractions—then the love of his father could have dawned upon him.

Where was the elder brother to start but there? Where are we? I find there are some people I just don't even want to acknowledge as brothers, let alone go out of my way to know and understand. We will probably never have compassion and concern and understanding for the listless, unlovely, and the loser until *first, we are overwhelmed with the love the Father has for us.* That's what breaks me!

If we dare to believe that we are restored in fellowship with God our Father just because he loves us and that we are responsible in our own lives as a result, we should have such gratitude that it takes us far beneath the surface of the problems of people.

When I realize I have been given a second chance and don't deserve it and, in fact, have received a third and fourth and hundredth chance with God, I am almost forced to rejoice that others can have a second.

But there is *a fundamental principle to the Christian faith* that is missed by this story, since it was a parable with only one primary teaching focus. It is the principle missed in attitudes of many toward the growing burden of welfare in our day. It is a unique fundamental which has grown in our American experiment of social government. *It is the supreme worth of the individual.* This is at the heart of much of our jurisprudence, and is the motivational force in medicine and medical research. And the church can be the one institution which does not let America forget. Furthermore, the church is the one sociological grouping that places a supreme value on each individual just because he *is.*[1]

We know we must produce. Faith without works is dead. *But the declaration of our faith is that we are significant to God and, therefore, should be to each other, regardless of any utilitarian purpose.* This is what welfare says. This is what the right to subsistence says. This is what a guaranteed annual income says. Regardless of any utilitarian purpose, each individual has worth.

Because of what we believe God has done, how much more do we claim this for others. "For God so loved the world that he gave his only son" (John 3:16). I forget the extravagance of that fact! We all forget its explicit demand on us! "For God sent the Son into the world, not to condemn the world, but that the world might be saved through him" (John 3:17). What that does to my sometimes petty attitudes! Greater worth has no one than for someone to lay down his life for them. How that dwarfs my style of concern! How about you?

Remember, a parable's purpose is to teach a single truth. You do it injustice to read into it ideas other than those intended by the author. But I can't help thinking of *what Jesus would say about the situation if the younger son had not shaped up?* What should the older, responsible brother have thought? For this is more nearly the truth of many situations which you and I face. I am thinking particularly of a family where there were also two sons. But in this case it was in reverse. The older brother had been the irresponsible one, flunking out of two schools, drinking heavily, and leaving for weeks without so much as a good-bye. The mother of the family had a bad heart and each time the son left, everyone feared she would die of sorrow and anxiety.

It was the younger son who took over the family business and played the responsible role. The entire family was used and abused by this older son. But with deep Christian as well as family love, they kept the door open, hopes high and forgiveness renewed until the tragic death of the fellow, still unreformed.

Somehow this experience must be the vision God has for each of us—the door is open to the end. I cannot help but believe Jesus could have told this parable in a different way to point up another truth—the son does *not* come to himself. He just returns. The father in this version also runs down the road while his son is still far from the house, robe flying, arms outstretched; and the ring, the robe, the fatted calf, and the party all follow.

The surprised, resentful older brother returns and finds out what is happening. He complains in the same way, "Look how many years I have slaved for you and never disobeyed a single order of yours and yet you have never given me as much as a young goat so that I could give my friends a dinner! But when that son of yours arrives, who has spent all your money on prostitutes, for him you kill the calf we got ready for market."

And I can imagine Jesus putting on the lips of the father, as the words of God to each of us,

> My dear son, you have been with me all the time and everything I have is yours. But we *had* to celebrate and show joy. For this is your brother; I thought he was dead—but he *is* alive! I thought he was gone for good, but there is still hope— Rejoice in your brother—and the possibility.

A friend of mine was sharing with me the desperate straits people can get into that others hardly know about. Yet there is that undiscovered potential when people take time to care.

It came to her attention that a little elderly woman from another congregation (in fact, from another denomination there in her town) was starving to death, destitute in a small, dark, one-room apartment. The local pastor of the old woman had done little to champion her cause in getting her into a denominational rest-home. Most rest-homes demand entrance fees, and she was old, penniless, and could contribute nothing. So my friend went over, met the woman, and began to scheme how *she* could secure help to get her into a home. This vibrant socialite with country club interests and activities, church responsibilities and commitments, took time to rejoice in the personhood of a little, old, destitute stranger.

In making the arrangements, my friend started helping the woman sort out her things. They began going through books and papers. She discovered that the woman had saved Christmas cards over the years. The old lady was now very forgetful, and my friend was in for an amazing discovery. The woman had made it her practice when receiving money as a Christmas gift—and other monies—to stick it in the Christmas cards and leave it there. Probably through her senility she had forgotten about it. When my friend gathered and counted all the money, she found the woman had $12,000—more than enough to pay her way into a home and keep her comfortably for the rest of her days. She was literally starving to death with riches at her fingertips!

What riches might be stored away in the lives of our brothers, waiting to be uncovered by someone who cares enough to look beneath the surface?

"It is fitting to make merry and be glad," even in the potential of our brother.

7

Celebration
Through Preferring Others

I received bad news, and yet it invoked a prayer of thanks. An elder I love like a father and brother in Christ, who shared adventures with me in prayer, outreach to others and friendship, had a coronary and had been in intensive care in the hospital in my former hometown.

Together we had championed into life a non-profit housing corporation to help those having problems because of discrimination. We had shared a deep vision for Christ, expressing his love through people.

Then at a meeting I had further documentation of what I already knew as Sam's way. The day before his heart attack, Sam had been to a long and tiring meeting which lasted into the evening. It was then he found out about the problem of another attendee of that meeting, a woman who had been burned out of her apartment. He stayed late in the night, calling all over New York, assisting her in finding an apartment. The next morning he was hospitalized.

This is typical of Sam, someone who is so filled with the love of Christ, so turned on by him for the needs of others, that he prefers them to himself.

It occurred to me that his coronary is a red badge of love, a decoration of commitment, a medal given for service, a signpost of preferring others to himself. Some might say Sam is a very ordinary man. But those who know him know a very special human because he has discovered the ex-

71

traordinary joy of preferring others, of celebrating his neighbor.

Waiting for dinner to be served in a hotel lobby at another meeting that week, I heard a famous personality being interviewed on one of those guest shows. This was a beautiful singer who told of a serious disease which had threatened her with disfigurement, almost taking her life. She said such an experience made her appreciate what is most important in life. The TV host was sharp and caught that. He asked her what that was. What was important to her now? How disappointing it was that out of her near-death experience, which pressed her to sort out ultimate values, her insight was no more than a she-wolf for her cubs. Her answer—her children. Not eternal values or the worth of humanity in its throbbing need around her; nothing beyond the natural love relationships of family. She still lived in the realms of self-concern.

Jesus broke open a new understanding of human relationships that seems difficult to understand, unless you know him. Sam has discovered it and gives himself away to others. A beautiful singer misses it and stays confined to the orbit of her own life.

The secret is wrapped up in Jesus Christ. He became the divine power to release men from the tyranny of themselves, to discover the joy of preferring others.

Recently I talked to a young man who displayed a keen mind, exceptional vocabulary, and an awareness of some of the major philosophical approaches to life, but who had rejected Christ as having any substance of reality and who thinks primarily of himself. I was curious about how this well-informed, apparently confident young man felt, and I asked him if he were happy. I wasn't surprised to find he wasn't.

My reflection on it, which I shared with him, was that there was a time when I thought I had everything under control in my life also. But I neither cared about people nor was I happy. As a matter of fact, except for the invasion of God into my life, I probably would care very little about others now. That young man would not have received the time of day from me. But he *was* getting the time of day and as much of me and my life and friendship as he wanted because Christ has given me a reason for celebrating others and preferring them. I cannot brag about it because I didn't do it. God did it for me. But I certainly can witness to the joy that comes out of it!

It is no new news that the world has deteriorated into camps of bitterness, loneliness, and in quarters alien to the clear understanding of most of us, into armed violence and revolution. It is no news that people of various persuasions and motivations are trying to do something about the problems of people individually and as groups. The church shares no unique calling in evoking this kind of personal care, individual for individual, group for group. But it IS news—*new* news every time—when individuals are so aware of God's love for them that they understand their true self-worth. It isn't in egotistical pride to be consumed in pleasure but in the worth of personhood. It *is* news when they turn outward on life to see the worth of every human in the very same way.

It is news—*new* news every time—when they demonstrate they really know *that* as the Good News of God by preferring others to themselves. When people prefer others' pleasure to their own pleasure, or time, or financial holdings, or security, safety, or privileged cultural advantage, something *is* different.

Somehow a great, vast host of good people across the United States naïvely think this tragically divided world is just going to mend somehow and things are going to get back to something called normal. What is "normal" will never return. The problems will not, as one person so sincerely but naïvely told me, fade away.

The unique conviction the church has to proclaim, and should but often does not, is this—a divine power has become Person for this very reason. This person, Jesus Christ, has come to meet man's needs directly, squarely, transformingly, *within us and between us!* We are to proclaim it by incarnating it in every man, woman, and child who has dared take the wonderful name of Jesus on his lips. *The miracle will be known when we prefer others.* When it happens, it is convincing. The result is the joy of celebrating another.

But how does it happen? *First,* I think *by attitude.* Staying overnight with friends while on a speaking engagement in a neighboring state, this became clear in the attitude I sensed they had. This couple are people you are cheated for not having known. They are attractive, warm, gracious, sensitive, and caring. My hostess told me of keeping an Indian Moslem in their home as part of a Rotary program of hosting people from overseas. One morning the Indian gentleman came down a bit early for breakfast, and she was not quite ready. So she handed him a pamphlet which simply explained the central truth and power of the Christian faith, and said, "You might like to read this as I finish getting breakfast ready." He took it up to his room and moments later came down quite excited and said that this was the first time in three years in America that any Christian had shared his faith with him.

An attitude of sensitivity toward others, caring about them in the light of what we believe, is the very new and good news about Christ.

On the way out to the airport, Bob, her husband, told me another story, this time of the previous year when they had been host again. This time it was for a mutual friend of ours who was a hospital chaplain. His name is George.

When George was getting ready to leave, he suddenly said he had the feeling that instead of taking a plane home, he should take a bus and asked his host, Bob, to drive him to the bus terminal. When they arrived, Bob decided to check into the prayer and meditation room he had helped establish at the terminal. It is manned twenty-four hours a day by laymen. When he arrived, a man was on duty, reading a Bible. But he had a terribly distressed look on his face. Bob asked him if anything was wrong and discovered the young man was severely depressed, at the point of almost total despair. Bob rushed back to George and told him he knew why he had been guided to take a bus instead of a plane. George found a young fellow on the verge of suicide and, with trained expertise, dealt with his specific need.

Again and again God tunes us into the needs of others if Jesus Christ has captured our lives. For he came to sensitize us to others. He came as the very incarnation of God's attitude toward men. God's love makes our own use of the term almost cheap by comparison. God's love, which Jesus expressed, was sensitivity to the dilemmas of man. It was availability. It was holding up the divine possibilities of people.

John the Baptist caught the significance of what preferring others was to mean almost immediately. Filled by the Holy Spirit, he put the life-style into a model for us,

> This joy of mine is now full . . .
> He must increase and I must decrease . . .
> > (John 3:30)

We laugh and mildly scold our children when they each try to jockey the other out of position in order to get the largest piece of chocolate cake for themselves. But later on they will be manipulating another out of position for the promotion they want for themselves in the corporate structure. Industry would be dramatically influenced by a new ethic if Jesus Christ became the predominant force in the lives of executives and if John the Baptist became a model for this attitude, finding joy in preferring another.

What might happen to a company where each executive, especially the middle echelon, each superintendent and foreman, tried to outdo the other in encouraging each other and making the other look good, instead of the present practice? Impossible? Yes, I think it is—*apart from Christ!*

I tell children they will be reaching some recognizable maturity—something some adults never reach—when they begin to truly want their sister or brother, or the kid down the street, to have the largest piece of chocolate cake. That's the joy of preferring one another. To see the divine possibility in them and live with that attitude toward them is celebrating the life of your neighbor.

Think of the people Jesus met. What was our Lord's attitude toward the woman at the well of Samaria? Did he see in her anybody's woman, or a life-giver carrying good

news, symbolized in his request to have her give him a cup
of cold water?

He saw in Peter not a vulgar fisherman, but the rock of
faith as a model for all of Christianity; in Zacchaeus not
a traitor to Israel, but a man in mission; in an adulteress not
a sinner, but a freed woman released to sin no more.

His attitude toward you? Not what you once were, but
what you are to be! For now you are to be the incarnation
of that same attitude for others, *seeing in them the divine
possibilities, claiming the same hope, being sensitive to the
same opportunities.* Any thinking white person should immediately ask, however, "What about the black militant
threatening me? How can I celebrate that person, much
less prefer him?" Nothing more clearly illustrates the
stance Jesus struck in his life for us. The white man must
realize that, for the present, many blacks must write their
own agenda, and whites must wait and be ready as we are
invited—if invited we will be. The joy of Jesus Christ will
be in preferring them. It will be in celebrating their own
cultural uniqueness and individuality, their racial beauty
and divine possibilities on their own terms and ways under
God, not through our white filters of quasi-truth. At the
same time, in an age when blacks have more leverage than
ever before in history and when they must for their own
good and ours use that leverage for justice, Jesus Christ also
incarnates for them God's attitude of preferring others. If
they are not to wither in bitterness or fail in the midst of
their success, they must discover the joy of celebrating the
divine possibilities in the white community, which is still so
filled with the subtle and the obvious discriminations and
the built-in injustices. As blacks claiming justice, they too
must prefer others by giving mercy.

If Jesus Christ came as the incarnation of the living
God's attitude toward his creatures, more profoundly he
came *as God's actions for men.*

If God had remained with us only at the point of awareness and sensitivity we would still live in darkness—searching for revelation, groping along for rules to keep. But God
acted! The Word became flesh. Love took on historical situa-

tion. Our words so often remain only words. Our love remains, like the singer we mentioned earlier, within the circle of our self-concern.

My love could be more extravagant. How about yours? But God put his all out there, to bleed and tear itself open to everyone on a cross. Jesus preferred others all the way. Whatever difficult, hard-to-understand justice was satisfied through the cross, it was for others to have their chances. "He must increase . . . " Whoever that might be and under whatever circumstances it might occur, John the Baptist could say, "but I must decrease."

Measure your life, your attitudes, your relationships, your use of time against that formula!

I have been aware of how quietly, almost imperceptibly, people can change. Looking back, I can see how it has happened in my own life, and I see the difference in people I meet everywhere. Attitude and action finally become a posture of life. You begin to know what Jesus was about in life. You become more meaningful to yourself as you help life be more meaningful for others. If there was ever an example of being an advocate of others, that's what Jesus was. He modeled what we are to be. And you can tell those who are living his life out in his way! Most of us could probably quote John 3:16, but the verse following is crucial to understanding the meaning of God's strategy in taking on human form in Jesus. On Calvary his role of advocate for us in full self-sacrifice has never been more fully understood or critically needed than today. The disadvantaged, and underprivileged need advocates who, like Jesus, incarnate God's attitude of love by action.

"He must increase, but I must decrease." This might be the *only* formula for bridging the gaps and avoiding the violent clashes, and we saw it at work in the '60's. To salute the powerless and needy and support them will be the preference of joy which will make itself immune from easy, unrealistic proposals until men receive justice, hope, and dignity.

Possibly the reason we have never experienced the exhilaration of such joy is simply that our commitment to

Christ might not have taken us far enough beyond the safe security of our personal preferences to the point of personal abandonment.

Henry was senior pastor of a large and rather affluent suburban church in Chicago. He has been a warm, evangelical guy who believes Christian love must be incarnated in practice. So he has been clear and bold about political issues and racial justice. He says he felt general support even in his boldest proclamations on social justice. But then an issue for which there seemed to be no break-through came up in the community, and demonstration and confrontation seemed the only recourse. Hank moved out and led the protest march. He hoped to give encouragement to his fellow pastors, too, since by salary and prestige he had more to lose than many of the others.

He said he was shocked at the reaction of people who had previously glowed over his *verbal* stands. His "action-preaching" was condemned. His long-time secretary could hardly speak to him. His chief custodian, who had been with him in prayer and fellowship to start each day at the church, met him in the hall and said, "Oh, Doctor, how could you do such a thing?"

Abandonment of ourselves, going beyond rhetoric to action, is risky—and necessary—if the world is to hear and understand. "For God sent the Son into the world, not to condemn the world, but that the world might be saved through him" (John 3:17). God's strategy was not condemnation but affirmation!

This was the life-style of our lord, now to be incarnated in us. But what so often happens when we are confronted with people and situations upsetting to us is that we either degrade them to bolster our own ego-security or we flatter them to manipulate them. I constantly fight slipping back into that old way of acting. I know how I react and feel when someone affirms me. I remember a disagreement with a man on our board over an issue on which I knew he and I would take a different stand. But it demanded a vote on one of those yes-or-no, winners-losers issues. What a great feeling, what a gift to me it was when he affirmed me after the meeting, after firmly clarifying his continued disagreement. What that affirmation did was to recognize my divine worth.

An articulate black friend, Bill Pannell, writes in his book *My Friend, the Enemy* [1] that if we are to be his friends, we owe it to him to fight for clarity, to force honesty, to allow neither rage nor despair as escapes from gaining clarity in communication, even if it means risking hurt at times.

We make the mistake of thinking affirmation means agreement. No, it means caring enough to challenge and clarify, but also listening and being honest. Thus you will indicate the other person is important enough for you to search out the reasons for your differences.

In Tennessee Williams's *Cat on a Hot Tin Roof*, Brick is unwilling to face up to himself and tries the old unsatisfactory route of liquor. His trouble with his wife, father, and his work is the same thing he is going through with other people. Toward the end of the play his father, Big Daddy, who really is concerned about his boy, keeps after him. He will not be turned aside by the evasions and rationalizations the son tries to use to protect himself from confrontation. Whatever he says, Big Daddy keeps after him, suffering through the inevitable pain that comes when we keep after the truth with another person. Finally there is a break-through and the boy is won back to sanity and restored relationships.

Dr. Reuel Howe points out that most people miss the point of such a play. Such crude realities as the play portrays easily offend so many. "It is a shame," he says, "that we would rather be pretty than redemptive. We seem to place respectability above salvation." [2]

The wholeness of others, like the wholeness we want to claim for ourselves, will come through a new attitude we have toward every other human. This attitude is the result of the invasion of Jesus Christ into our lives, giving us, as Paul puts it, "another point of view" of people—loved under God as much as God has loved us, forgiven even as we have been forgiven, with divine possibilities held out to them the same as they have been held out to us.

The wholeness for people will come when we implement this new attitude with action, affirming them, even by caring enough to break through to significant meaning beyond differences, resistance, and even hatred. We must decide if we would rather be pretty than redemptive. It might mean caring enough to pursue the ugly children of our society's own making. It might mean playing the sometimes thankless role of an advocate for those we would not prefer, let alone love. One couple opened their home to youth, losing the privacy they preferred. It has been a great ministry, befriending many teenagers. But one set of parents sued this couple for alienating their child from them. All they had done was to take him in, accept and love him, often at the costly expense of their sleep and schedules. Finally they prayed to have the cup of abuse and persecution lifted. But what fulfilled people! They are still working in depth with teenagers, paying the price, struggling with the mixed potion of trouble and joy!

The truth is, there is joy in preferring others, the joy Jesus said he had which would be ours. He incarnated it in his life-style and claimed it for all of us who follow him. This is the joy of celebrating others!

8

Can Suffering
Be a Cause to Celebrate?

"It is part of the comforting creed of millions that they can avoid all suffering, satisfying their appetites and live in a continual round of self-indulgence. Though few can succeed long at this enterprise, some succeed for a while, but they have their reward! They seek the superficial and they get it, but they miss all that makes life transcendentally lovely!" [1]

★ ★ ★

"Let him deny himself and take up
his cross and follow me . . ."

★ ★ ★

A small group of women was studying the Bible in our church parlor. I walked in on them, and they asked, "Do you 'give thanks in all things' and 'rejoice in your suffering'?" I don't like pretense and so I had to admit, "No, I hate suffering!" I have a great deal to learn about this problem. In comparison with some, I've had my small share of suffering. But I talked with a POW who survived seven years of torture and internment in North Vietnam and realized I know little of suffering on that scale. If we suffer to any degree, our perspective will be clarified and possibly redeemed if we put it in the framework of what Christ said and did. It might not speak directly to the trials of a bad marriage, a continual physical ailment that causes extreme pain, or some other personal suffering

81

you are experiencing. But the perspective might change it all.

It must have been a frightening, traumatic moment when Jesus smashed the dreams of Peter and the rest of the disciples. They had been with him up to then. They had come to believe God was moving in a very special way in Jesus' life, that he was *the* Anointed One Israel had waited for to lead them into a new kingdom.

He had strange power to heal, a charismatic personality to capture the imagination of the crowds and inspire them to faith and discipleship, and unique insight into the mysteries of God's will that made the complicated seem simple and possible for ordinary men.

Jesus moved the strangest persons to faith—untouchable tax collectors, prostitutes, beggars, and thieves. He matched wits with the cleverest Temple scribes and squared off with the wisest and most awesome of the Pharisees. He moved easily in and out of deep conversations and casual, happy relationships at a party, to great solitude in prayer all night long. As if he had the very authority of God, he forgave sins and made pronouncements on the will of God and the actions of men. And then he talked of suffering and death!

It was not that the disciples were strangers to either. They had risked their lives on more than one occasion, and they had all suffered to some degree or another. But if anyone should be spared tragedy, it was this man with whom they had shared life the past few months and for whom they had come to have such a deep reverence and regard. But he said suffering was around the corner for him. Then of all things, Jesus said that suffering would be at the hands of the religious leaders who had completely misread and misunderstood his mission, method, and ministry. And death —he said he had to die!

Peter said it just shouldn't happen! It was wrong to be talking that way. Jesus had too much to live for; he had too much to do! Jesus meant too much to them! No! It would never happen!

Jesus' response surprised them. "That's the devil's talk, Peter. Get out of the way, for you're a roadblock to the very purpose of my life. Talking that way you are on Satan's side. You are thinking in men's terms, not God's."

Those men were shocked at this turn of the conversation, this shattering of their dreams of Jesus going on to greater and greater triumphs until all Israel and the world understood and followed him. He told them what the further implications of the future were. If any man was to be a disciple of his in the future, it would mean obedience, personal self-denial and his own cross! For if they had any idea of a comfortable, successful road ahead, they were mistaken! They could protect themselves but lose the whole significance of the calling he had held out to them. Or they could abandon themselves to him and his cause, lose their lives in mission and find themselves! For them it was the clearest delineation of not only their call but also of the unmistakable demands of it, which they had heard. It was the point of departure for their ministry and for the discipleship of all the millions who would follow their example, with precise demand, so no one would ever be confused again—

> self-denial,
> cross and obedience,
> the cost of caring!

These were the terms of discipleship! Hard terms! We need to understand them. If membership in the church is inaugurated by confession of Jesus Christ as Lord and a commitment to discipleship, then one wonders how many of the millions who joined the church ever understood the meaning of what they said and committed themselves to, which Jesus so clearly stated and lived out by purposely allowing himself to be killed. But I wouldn't be any different from Peter. I would also suggest expediency, concession, a different strategy to save his life for a longer ministry.

How does this suffering and death really figure in? How can we be positive about this and celebrate our own sufferings, not in masochism, but in responsible and creative living? For it is obvious that Jesus was not a negative person. He validated life and said his mission was to see all men have real life and experience it in abundance! Suffering isn't something I naturally consider as a part of abundant living!

The kind of joy Jesus knew of wholeness and purpose, dignity and fulfillment, he coveted for all men. He offered an inner peace which could result from an integrated personality. He wanted to make the lives of the sick, lost, and debilitated sing with meaning.

But for those who would not only claim the Christian life, but would also become agents for his spirit to capture the imagination and wills of others, there was only one way. He spelled it out. This is the cost of celebrating life in Jesus Christ, the cost of caring and the answer to the question I raised earlier—the key is suffering which is redemptive.

I think the first step in discipleship is self-denial which becomes self-affirmation.

Now, be careful on this and read me correctly. There was a time when I over-simplified this step and laid an almost impossible demand on people. God wonderfully forgives us for our mistakes, and we can be grateful that he takes us on to further maturity. I had believed that becoming a committed disciple of Jesus Christ meant you must die to yourself. How often Christian writers and preachers had made this point in my early Christian growth!

But I was leading a weekend of renewal for a Pittsburgh church a few years ago, and before one of my presentations, when I was going to lay this idea before them, I went into the men's room to spruce up. Standing before the mirror, combing my hair and straightening my tie, I suddenly realized (Could it not have been Christ talking to me?). "B. Jay—here you are, ready to tell others about death of self and ego and you're all self-concerned about how you look! Why, you haven't died to *yourself!* But you're not supposed to! It's a matter of dying to the *right* of yourself."

I had a big laugh at myself and went out and began my talk with a sharing of my new revelation, so clear to me now! We can never forget ourselves, nor should we. If we did, we would be irresponsible for our personal health, social graces, and personal commitments. If we died completely *to* ourselves, we would be unable to love our neighbors *as* ourselves.

The hope for our souls is not to have our egos obliterated. It is the matter of who is running our "computers," the ego —the almighty "I"—or our Lord! This is where Jesus' call to discipleship has been misunderstood. The act of sacrifice for Lent is typical. Denial, going without things, has been used to heighten appreciation and prove commitment. But, as William Laws once wrote,

> Self-denials do only that which indulgences do for other people; they withstand and hinder the operation of God upon their own souls and, instead of being really self-denials, they strengthen and keep up the kingdom of the self.

I remember one man in a former church who attempted to be faithful to all he considered responsible Christian commitment—regular worship, tithing, work in the church, honesty and integrity in his business life. But he had an old blue Plymouth that belched blue smoke from the exhaust and was rusted through in several spots. I suspected he could have afforded a little bit better and more economical car to run. But he kept that car like a sign of self-denial, drawing curious inquiries constantly, to which he could respond proudly about how he was denying himself.

It is ironic that in a world of need, we are tyrannized by "things." Some hardly realize they have rejected the kingdom of God and become part of the kingdom of thingdom, their lives built around and dependent on the material.

But don't misunderstand and miss the real significance of what Jesus is saying. Denial of self as one of the demands of discipleship is not a rejection of material things. The object of the verb in "let him deny himself" is a direct object, not an indirect object. He is *not* to deny *something to* himself, but he is to *deny himself*. The Greek of the original text means "to refuse," "to renounce," "to abandon"—it means abdication! God desires an *abdication of our own right of will in opposition to God, and the affirmation of Christ as Lord of our lives*, which becomes affirmation of a new "us."

For "denial" so often means a negation. I believe it is ultimately the great positive. The joy and the power that comes through affirmation of Jesus Christ as being in charge of all you feel and think, strive for and desire is denial through affirmation, a step to discipleship!

But is our suffering "the cross we have to bear"? This archaic language is familiar but misunderstood. We have heard so many sermons on the subject that there is little that is new which I can offer. But it isn't the freshness of an idea we need. It is the freshness of what Jesus meant in our own personal experience that we need to claim. What does "taking up your *cross*" mean?

There are two perversions of this idea. One is characteristically heard from those who are sick in some way. They speak of having to bear their "crosses." Personal human suffering through some of these physical struggles, while we would all avoid them, *can* have a redemptive quality to the experience. How many have grown in stature, matured in insight, and become appreciative of health and life, because of their own struggle through sickness? But this is not what Jesus meant by "taking up your cross."

The other way this idea is often misused is when someone has a difficult situation he must endure—a family problem, a station in life, a loved one for whom he must care. He calls the situation his "cross." But the cross of discipleship is something else. The criminal of Jesus' day carried his own cross to the place of execution, and it was an instrument of severe, excruciating, and torturous death. He was stretched on the cross, legs broken, to hang while his own body-weight suffocated the breath out of him.

Jesus purposely chose this image to illustrate the complete commitment we are to make to him. *The cross we each are to take up is the willingness to accept the consequences of total commitment to God and his will for humanity, as well as for ourselves*. It is faithfulness to the point of being a criminal, a social outcast if the circumstances so develop, even to the point of personal death. Nothing, even life itself, is to stand in the way. God doesn't put us on a cross. The world does.

It means responding positively to what the world and life lays on us because we are resolutely God's man or woman! The cross Jesus was forced to face and die upon was laid on him not because he sang "God is love" and "For he's a jolly good fellow." He was nailed to the tree because he sang out for the world to hear, "The religious leaders are like white-washed tombs!"—"Thieves in the temple!"—"Let justice and mercy flow down like a mighty river!" He disturbed and challenged the status quo which protected those living comfortably off the inequities and injustices of their system and exposed the good and religious people who did nothing about it.

If *celebrate* means "to act out publicly," to "demonstrate to all," then there are crosses to be picked up in our day again, if God's will is to be celebrated! Those crosses must not be left by default to radical revolutionaries who would destroy our American experiment in order to attempt curing its ills. Those crosses must be picked up by God's people who believe justice must be tempered with love, reform with spiritual renewal, and caring paid with whatever price is demanded.

Anyone sensitive at all feels his heart go out to the suffering millions on this planet. So much so that in the face of the immensity of it all, the monstrous montage of human agony from starvation, poverty, disease, sorrow, inhumanity of man to man, more than one has been moved to cry out, "How can there be a God who could allow this?"

Albert Schweitzer did not repudiate God in the face of suffering but struck his life on the anvil to be shaped into an instrument to help meet the need.

> Whoever among us has through personal experience learned what pain and anxiety really are . . . belongs no more to himself alone; he is the brother of all who suffer.

This is part of the cost of caring. If we are to talk about

celebrating life, we must realistically face the untold suffering which is part of daily human experience. We will identify with it, suffer anguish with those who are in anguish, enter into it, and pick up our crosses if need be!

So these two qualities are set in the center of all that it means to be a Christian, denying the right to our self in preference to Christ's life and will expressed through us, and so entering into the needs of the suffering world that God can lay a cross on us. Whatever else we have wanted to believe was part of the story must be set aside until this is settled. Self-denial and cross-bearing. We will never be able to celebrate, affirm, or enjoy all that God meant for us until we know we are ready for this to be true for us. It will put our other personal sufferings in the right perspective.

As it now reads, there are only two factors—self-denial and willingness to bear our crosses! But what about the matter of *following?* Is it a third requirement if we are to understand celebrating suffering? No! This is the conditional part of what Jesus said, *the result of self-denial and cross-bearing.* Yet knowing that, we could well consider it as a third condition, out of our own self-examination. For what of our obedience and self-discipline? Probably not one of us is as disciplined in our faith as we could be! *We don't follow as we could!*

Albert Day writes in a wonderful little book entitled *Discipline and Discovery.*

> We Protestants are an undisciplined people. Therein lies the reason for much dearth of spiritual insight and serious moral power . . . Without discipline there would have been no Francis of Assisi, no Bernard of Clairvaux, no Teresa of Avila, no Brother Lawrence, no William Laws, no Evelyn Underhill, no Thomas Kelly . . .[2]

Many of us probably don't even recognize these names, because, with the exception of a few Olympic gold-medalists, disciplined lives are no longer the heroes for today. Rather, it is the self-indulgent imprisoned by their needs, dictated to by their passions, that fire the imagination of so many in the world. Bishop Fulton J. Sheen was right several years ago.

> Moral force is like running water in a narrow channel. It rushes forward to the field where it is to dispense fertility, but it must have barriers to confine its energies and direct its course. The difference between a swamp and a river is that the swamp has no banks.

If discipline and obedience are denials of some of our appetites and passions, in a much greater way they are still affirmations of our goals and our Lord. They indicate our willingness to become channels for the moral and spiritual force of God through us.

Frankly, in the 1960's I was impressed by the abandonment of some of our younger generation to pay the price of physical discomfort, mob violence, police brutality, establishment hostility, public ridicule, beatings, imprisonment and, in a few cases, even death, for the cause of their social convictions. I was not necessarily sympathetic to their every cause nor convinced they thought through the full implications of radical and sometimes untenable conclusions. Nor am I supportive of violence as a means to their end. But their abandonment to a cause is attractive!

Is Albert Day a pious old square of a lost generation? Is he out of it, or does he reflect a singularly important secret at the heart of what Jesus held out to us? What the church and world need primarily is not more organization and program and money. What it needs

> Now, as always is the presence within it of a few God-conscious, God-centered souls. Even a few here and there would mean very much to a church confronted by the chaos of this age.
>
> A multitude of men and women, pressing on to the mark for the prize of the high calling of God in Christ Jesus, would confront the secularism and scepticism of our time with a challenge not easily laughed off or shunted aside. True holiness is a witness that cannot be ignored.[3]

Linus says to Charlie Brown in one cartoon sequence from *Peanuts*, "When I get big, I'm going to be a real fanatic." Charlie asks, "What are you going to be fanatical about, Linus?" With a quizzical look on his face Linus reflects, "Oh, I don't know . . . it doesn't really matter . . . I'll be sort of a wishy-washy fanatic!" There are all too many of those in the world! Wishy-washy fanatics! But those who make a difference are all too few.

Doesn't it matter what we are zealously committed to? We were meant to celebrate life. So were many others who will never have a chance unless we become their advocates. But there is a cost of suffering, undoubtedly, in the process of our faithfulness. It might be even to death, the fanaticism that affirms in self-denial with Christ alone as Lord who calls us to radical obedience and service.

9

Celebrating Life
Even Facing Death

When my grandmother who helped raise me died, it was after a long illness in her elder years. She had been a wonderful friend to me and loved me and cared for me. Her last year in her illness and suffering had opened up some deep spiritual experiences, and I knew she was ready. I didn't cry.

But when my father died, as we left the cemetery, I broke down. The sense of irreversibleness overwhelmed me. We had known each other for only three years and had been together since our reconciliation only three times. I felt cheated—cheated of the years without a father, cheated, now that we had been reconciled, of the few warm later years of his life which we could have shared. It made me think more introspectively and appreciatively about the problem some have as I counsel with them about making the funeral service a time of celebration!

But trouble and death are parts of life, and ultimate tests for our faith.

How quickly the disciples affirmed *their* belief. But Jesus asked, "Do you *now* believe?" But would their belief stand the test? It would be their frightening experience to be scattered, that belief they were professing scarcely strong enough to hold them together when officers of the Temple arrived to arrest this one in whom they now so confidently affirmed belief.

Do you *now* believe? Oh, you do? How will it be with you when you are in the valley and trouble really tests you? Will the trouble come in a problem at work or in a friend in some social relationship? Could it even be an unkind word of someone in church, illness, or even the specter of death? The test will be that trouble. For those of you who have been or still are in the valley of life's trouble and trauma right now, you KNOW belief in Christ takes on entirely new proportions.

Is Christ really the power of God—the power of God for YOU? Jesus said, "In the world you have tribulation." The question is, "You believe now. Will it stand the test of tribulation?"

Now the truth of the matter is that there are some very strong individuals who happen to be Christians who hold up well under the worst of circumstances. They battle it out. People are liable to compliment them on their courage. "How well she has held up through it all!"

I've seen marvelous Christians broken in sorrow in their losses, or shattered in the disappointments of their lives, humanly weak and not holding up at all in grief. For all they said and did, their faith was missing one clear resolve, one sure hope, one almighty trust, that the person of Jesus Christ gives. For it is not human strength bolstered by Christian principles we need, but HIM. A great heresy has developed in the Christian church. It is so subtly subscribed to that we stand shocked to have it uncovered.

A program of actions has replaced for many belief in a person. Detective novelist Dorothy Sayers is no superficial thinker in her fiction-writing or in her faith, "That you cannot have Christian principles without Christ is becoming increasingly clear because their validity as principles depends on Christ's authority." For there is no Christianity without Christ. I am not talking about a once-upon-a-time author of a new code or an historical martyr of a cause or a concept of a creed, but about a living person!

A promise is no better than the power behind it to fulfill it. So it sounds like cheap advice when we hear said to worried men facing the tribulations of the world, "Be of good cheer." "Take courage!" "Hang in there, man!"

You have only to have been completely down some time and have had some cheery soul ring out lightly, "Cheer up," to be driven down the rest of the way. It would be cheap advice except for the SOURCE! Christ does not offer us consolation. He offers himself!

I'll never forget walking through a rain-soaked graveyard in London where Charles Wesley, Isaac Watts, and Daniel Defoe (author of *Robinson Crusoe*) are buried. Across the street in the home of John Wesley it was moving to kneel on a little wooden bench in the back room of a study, contemplating with tears in my eyes the great devotion and service of the man who had knelt there two hundred years before. But it is not the inspiration of such great men then or now which will get us through our own trials. Wesley, just before he died on March 2, 1791, opened his eyes and with a clear voice acclaimed, "The best of all is, God is with us."

". . . in me you may have peace. In the world you have tribulation; but be of good cheer, I have overcome the world" (John 16:33). It isn't in platitudes or principles, but in the person of Christ himself that we have the power of a victorious life through the tribulations we face. If our beliefs are inadequate in our trouble, it is not different beliefs we need but HIM! David Livingstone asked his students at Glasgow University, "Shall I tell you what sustained me amidst the toil and hardship, the loneliness of my exiled life? It was the promise, 'Lo, I am with you always, even unto the end.' " The promise is no better than the power of the fulfillment of it—the power of that peace and joy Christ offered us in himself!

Several years ago George Hagedorn, chief economist for the National Association of Manufacturers, called the attitude of businessmen toward the economic situation in which the nation found itself "looking over the valley." Considering the inflation, tight money, and very tenuous security of the economy, businessmen were borrowing against the future with the idea that it would cost more if they waited. He felt they were ignoring the approaching downward business adjustment which had to come. He believed they were naïve and unrealistic, "looking over the valley" of the present problems toward a future idealistic hope. At the present it looks as if he were wrong.

Facing some of the stark realities of life as we must, there is a longer view. It is looking "across the valley" of death. We all ultimately have death somewhere on the edges of our concern. We have other valleys, too—a loved one gone, disease or disaster snuffing out his life; a youngster who has rejected our love; an unfavorable medical report, blanketing a gray cloud over all we think or do; a dream smashed; a hope shattered; a joy gone out of our life; a marriage with the meaning eroding; a feeling of worthlessness settling over us. Real valleys to us. In those times, talk of joy or celebration seems naïve, trite, and worthless.

But no one can accuse Jesus of being naïve. Looking over his valley, somehow aware of the cruelty, pain, mocking, and death ahead of him, Jesus startled the awed disciples who were similar to us, "Take courage (be of good cheer); I have defeated the world!" He was trying to instruct simple men before the final crash of the curtain on the last act of the drama of his earthly life. And he got through! They understood! They blurted out their belief that he came from God! They believed—yes! They believed—just like I have sometimes believed—with my mind in the sudden flash of understanding—with my emotions in some other moment when I am caught up in inspiration—with a new resolve, vowing again to be faithful. But with the whole being? With spirit-enlightened understanding? Belief which stands the test?

We share a vision "over the valley" that the disciples could not. For them the immediacy of their relationship to Jesus, the trouble ahead, and finally his arrest and crucifixion were singularly consuming. But before it all Jesus said what we can now understand, if only we can now appropriate it for ourselves. "Be of good cheer, *I* have overcome the world!" Life is worth celebrating, not because we are Pollyannas, nor because we have resolved ourselves to the suffering in the flesh until we inherit our pie-in-the-sky. Nor is it because we have now a program of living right. There is a Christian conviction which gives us reason to celebrate individually whatever comes. It's the same corporately, as the church looking historically at the world scene with all its ups and downs. Jesus Christ has overcome the world! The power of sin and death does not have control over us. That is good news in anyone's book! The problem is, so few really experience that kind of victory. It might be because they have believed in the author of a creed and not claimed a person who is power in life.

Difficulties are the tests of Christ alive, working his purposes out. The disciples could not see that, but Jesus knew and that was why he could encourage them.

One of my closest friends says, "The difficulties which tested my faith were tempering experiences which pressed me to grow in depth as a servant of Christ. I started the Christian life caught up in the adventure of being part of God's solution to the need of the world. The cost of discipleship came later. As the years have flown by Christ has been hammering out the person for others he wants me to be. My question now in tragedy or disappointment is 'Lord, what new thing can I learn in this?' My response in joy and success is, 'Lord, what are you seeking to have me discover of your love and all-sufficient power in this?' "

Can you thank God for trouble? Can you feel that tribulation is part of the adventure you have with God, where you are called to be part of the solution of the need of the world? Can *you* believe Christ has overcome your world, and now you can discover what he wants to teach you through each situation? If *your* world is not yet overcome and conquered, then there is good news for you. Cheer up! Christ will overcome it for you, and you can have his peace!

I have always marvelled at a changed man, whose faith was apologetic and weak at one time and who was dependent on personal goodness and strength. Then he says he came to know Christ. One can actually see a new attitude of the person toward himself and others. You've seen them too—people newly alive and vital, hungry to worship, ready to be constructive and helpful, sensitive to the needs of others, and ready to learn better ways to share their faith with others. The difference between the belief of their for-

mer selves and their new lives is revealing. Somehow before
they believed only with a part of themselves, with a mind
subscribing to an idea. Then they came to believe with their
beings, having seen for themselves.

It is Mary weeping at the tomb contrasted with Mary
running back to the others crying out, "I have seen the
Lord!" It is the disciples despondent in the upper room
compared with the disciples seeing him for themselves and
trying now to convince Thomas. Since few men have ever
been able to claim actual visions of Christ, how can we
understand this? What can we say for the difference between one man turned off, ineffective, defeated by his problems, and another man with the same problems but turned
on, caring and learning God's purpose from each problem?
Isn't it that the latter man has caught an understanding,
beyond creed and Golden Rule, of the power of God? All
through history the witness is that it is Christ himself
meeting men where they are in daily life so that they feel
filled by his spirit.

This man does not want to try to make it alone any
longer. He sees that at best his finest hours are jaded. He
knows with all the intelligence with which his creator endowed him that in the crucial tests he can crack and fall
apart. He catches the spirit of the whole Christian faith—
that God IS in the world—that Christ IS alive, *not then
but now*. And he tests a promise and finds it true and with
a power behind it—with a person behind it. And he commits himself—even at the expense of dying to his own
"rights." All that he knows of himself he gives with full resolve. He begins to live *believing*, and believing, *lives*, looking for Christ alive in daily relationships, even in trouble—
and so seeing the Lord! He has "SEEN" the resurrected
Lord! *He* has been resurrected himself! He can celebrate life
even through the death of his willfulness, discovering that
the victory is a real one which Christ won in overcoming the
world. The resurrection of a dead man is a miracle only
God can perform. But the resurrection of a dead man is a
miracle only each of us as dead men can allow!

Belief? Do you believe now? What tribulation and trouble might you face in your personal life this coming year? Will you stand the test? Are *you* resurrected? Take your greatest strength and your greatest weakness as primary symbols of *you* and commit them fully to Christ's living lordship. The joy, the peace, the power is in Jesus Christ. What has come of his victory over the world will be seen in US, not just as a famous victory once, but for *you* now, and *in* you forever!

Jesus is alive! That is why we can celebrate, even in the face of tragedy and death. He lives and as he lives, you shall live also. Be of good cheer. Be his! Celebrate!

> Underneath, in darkness there was DEATH,
>> an ever-wasting emptiness,
>> an overwhelming nothingness,
>> a world-negating void.
> But chancing, risking, gambler-like,
>> LIFE cast into the void the seed of LIFE,
>> risking loss that gain might come,
>> burying seed in DEATH.
> And then the LIFE in light
>> called forth the seed from DEATH:
>> and (alleluia!) sprouting up,
>> a life to LIFE responded
>> struggled up—
>> up against
>> the world negating voice,
>> call-by-call growth,
>> leaf-by-leaf growth,
>> toward the call of LIFE in light,
>> back toward resurrection!
> DEATH, then, is nothing all-at-once;
>> in fact, it always was
>> all around us always by us,
>> overwhelming;
>> myriad its forms.
> DEATH is not what we are going to;
>> DEATH is what we're growing from:
>> slavery and violence,

the needed song not sung,
the wounded unhealed,
the love withheld,
the wonder undiscovered.
Everything that man should be,
yet has not ever been;
everything that man should do,
yet has not ever done;
every wrong instead of right,
every negative—partakes of DEATH,
is part of that relentless void,
that emptiness through which we grow
to reach the light of LIFE.
And, therefore, resurrection
is never all-at-once;
for we rise up day by day,
cell-by-cell growth,
leaf-by-leaf growth,
toward the light:
A child is born! And up we grow!
Lives—rebuilding after the ruin!
War is questioned (if not banished)!
Up we grow! Up we grow!
Now a poem! Sanitation! A skyscraper!
Up we grow!
Universal brotherhood, striving to be practiced!
There now, nations! Here a new drug!
Telstar sight and sound!
Up we grow! Growing, growing,
cell-by-cell growth,
leaf-by-leaf growth,
toward the light of resurrection!
CELEBRATE THE FEAST OF LIFE!!!!
HE IS RISEN!!!!
ALLELUIA!!!
WE ARE RISING!!!
ALLELUIA!!! [1]

10

Celebrating History

A shipwrecked sailor who had been stranded on a desert island for three years could hardly believe his eyes when one day he saw a ship on the horizon. When he signaled it stopped, dropped anchor, and a small boat came ashore. The officer stepped out and handed him a batch of newspapers. "The captain suggests," the startled marooned man was told, "that you read what's going on in the world. Then let us know if you still want to be rescued!"

But in a time like this I'm happy to be alive. I almost believe it is heretical *to not be* able to celebrate today. A heresy is a perversion of the accepted faith. The danger of heresy is that it misrepresents what was originally understood and bleeds it of its truth and power.

To say, "I wouldn't want to bring a child into a world like this," is as much a heresy as were the deism and naturalism of our forefathers in the first three centuries. That statement misunderstands our calling. For we were born for a time like this! Yes, for a time as bad as some presently believe it is!

Mark Twain, eternal pessimist, wrote to a friend, "I've been reading the morning paper. I do it every morning . . . well knowing that I shall find in it the usual depravities and baseness and hypocrisies and cruelties that make up civilization and cause me to put in the rest of the day pleading for the damnation of the human race."

One college philosophy professor recently wrote, "A vacuum has arisen in the Western world—a vacuum of conviction as to the way to meaning. At the moment there is no distinctive 'faith' possessing sufficient power to give drive and direction to our civilization."

Edward B. Lindaman, in his book, *Space: A New Direction for Mankind,*[1] states quite frankly, "Science is now remote not only from the church but from the mass of humanity. It talks incomprehensible jargon. The result is that the world has grown emptier for many people. Neither religion nor science speaks to them." He sees them with no visible goals except materialism and with an emptiness they can only fill with sex, drink, television, and travel. It is impossible to build a full life around an empty heart and an empty mind.

An oversimplification, perhaps? Possibly. But with a good deal of truth in it. In another place he observes, "Many officials speak of recent insurrections (the 1960 riots) in terms of doomsday. They say we have come to a time like the fall of Rome and the fall of the Bastille, when civilizations collapse because belief is dead." Then he quotes Lawrence M. Gold, president emeritus of Carlston College, who believes our civilization "will die when we no longer care." [2]

What do you think? Do you really care? Do you believe there is any hope for the present outcome of history? Do you give it any thought? Do you believe it makes much difference what you believe? Are you a pawn to circumstances? Do you have a responsibility for part of the historical process? How many of the events of life are touched by God? Can you celebrate history? I believe we can—and should—and I want to tell you why and how important I think it is.

The classic anchor for disbelief was again given to me in a recent conversation. "How can a loving God allow such evil and suffering to exist in the world?" What is your answer? I am sure you wouldn't pray with Samuel Clemens for the damnation of civilization, but the historical perspective of some isn't much better.

Lord Dunsamy frankly believes that "Humanity is like

people packed in an automobile which is traveling downhill without lights on a dark night at terrific speed and driven by a four year old child. The signposts along the way are all marked 'Progress'." Certainly, there is some cause to draw such a conclusion. Vice, repression, pollution, over-population, nuclear stockpiling and many other "attributes of our modern culture" seem to document his attitude. With the exception of one factor. God! The lord of history! We are children of hope because God is in control and we can celebrate history!

I suppose I would have despaired if I had been living in the time of the caesars of Rome. Would I have lived in the tradition and conviction of the Holy Spirit who has the strategy of history? Would that God have been a stranger to me? He wasn't to one old Jew, Simeon, who lived expectant that God guided his life (Luke 2:25–35). Remember the story? The Spirit brought Simeon to the Temple to reveal to him one of the turning points in history. Simeon walked by the Spirit, and his life conformed to his faith, and he was to celebrate an historical break-through. The Bible says, "This man was righteous and devout." Make of that what you want. Despise the pious self-righteous. Dismiss the religious show-offs. Deny those who claim exclusive insight and withdraw themselves from the common life. But this man lived a moral, worshipful life that in no way contradicted the opportunity for the Spirit of God to tune him in to God at work.

He believed he would see the Christ-event before he died—then this stirring to go to the Temple. Knowing no more than this inner compulsion, he went and felt directed to these strangers, a couple with an infant in their arms. A melody rose up within him as he took the baby in his arms,

> Now, Lord, you have kept your promise,
> and you may let your servant go in peace,

he poetically prayed.

> For with my own eyes I have seen your salvation,

which you have made ready in the presence of all peoples:
A light to reveal your way to the Gentiles,
And to give glory to your people Israel.

—Luke 2:29–33 (TEV)

Now that was a conviction that was wholly unjustified by all observable historical data. Jews even today would make the judgment this was a pious old deluded Jew. No glory for the Gentiles!

But listen! When Jesus Christ becomes contemporary, subjectively part of your experience, you know what Simeon felt. There might be an edge to your life that is frayed and frightening. But you can celebrate history too, because you can know God at work in the history of *your* being! You can know him at work in the arena of *your* life! If that isn't true, you might well join the pessimists of the day and hold on for dear life or hole up in fear.

We celebrate life because our eyes have seen, that is, we have known in our own experience that God of history has touched our own history in saving terms.

Simeon also said, "Which you have prepared for all your people." I am committed to a reconstructed society to political and economic justice and the non-violent revolution which will bring it about. It seems to me that this is a responsible interpretation of what Jesus meant for the impact of his life on the world when years later he interpreted his ministry to his home-town folks, "The Spirit of the Lord is upon me. He has anointed me to preach the Good News to the poor, He has sent me to proclaim liberty to the captives, And recovery of sight to the blind, To set free the oppressed, To announce the year when the Lord will save his people" (Luke 4:18–19, TEV).

But I feel so many fellow churchmen have abandoned an eternal and spiritual redemption of the world. They apologize for even the mention of Christ's name or of salvation in connection with social action. The leader of a denomination told me of a pastor who used to take students into a deep consciousness of evangelical concern for the world and then into work projects which implemented that con-

cern. In the midst of these projects he helped them learn
how to articulate their faith, and this executive said that
this pastor's program resulted not only in turned-on kids
but in changed lives of others through them. But he went
to a World Council of Churches seminar in Geneva, Switzer-
land. He came back changed. Now he bends over backward
to avoid ever mentioning Christ's name. It ends up as just
another humanistic brand of social work.

We celebrate history because we believe, as the old Welsh
hymn puts it, "God is working his purposes out." We celebrate history because he has given us an overview of history.
We dare to see his hand in the struggles for freedom and
justice in our day, even as corrupted and faulted as they
might be with the human factor. If devout and righteous
men do not opt out but prevail, what might we claim as
part of divine possibilities in God's permissive will in the
"major evolutionary emergence," as one person puts it?

In fact, it might be we are better humanists than the
humanists. Professor H. Evan Runner sees mankind at one
of history's turning-points. He declares the collapse of humanistic faith which believes man is lord of history. Our
new humanism sees salvation, wholeness in Jesus Christ
for all people with a new implication for man, a greater
sensitivity for the human needs of others. Contrary to the
old pious, church-oriented, religious imagery of this concern, salvation will be tough-minded for the realist. We
celebrate history, not by sitting back with a religious
fatalism, leaving the revolution to know-nothings.

John Gardner is a spokesman for change, although he is
no longer speaking in ivy-league surroundings as he did at
Harvard, but in the midst of a political morass in Washing-
ton. "The tasks of social change are tasks for the tough-
minded and competent. Those who come to the task with
the currently fashionable mixture of passion and incom-
petence only add to the confusion." [3]

The revolutionists of American colonial days are often
pointed to by contemporary radicals. But it is good to keep
in mind that our founding fathers had their lives founded
in a deep conviction of a moral code, in a basic political

concept upholding individual human rights as endowed with supreme and equal worth by their creator, and the encouragement of freedom of choice and corresponding personal responsibility *because God had authored it.*

We also celebrate history by our action. It should be our belief that God's will can be, must be, exercised by good and devout men, sometimes even through revolutionary processes, because of the inner revolution he has effected in us in Jesus Christ.

Harvey Cox has a responsible word for us, "But most importantly, prophecy sees everything in the light of its possibilities for human use and celebration. Without rejecting the influences of historical continuities, it insists that our interest in history, if it is not merely antiquarian, arises from our orientation toward the future . . . because we have a mission in the future." [4]

To understand the most profound reason of all for celebrating history, we need one of those $50 theological terms to express it. Eschatology! It means "having to do with last, final or future things . . . "

The salvation Simeon saw through the eyes of faith in the infant Jesus' birth was a vision of the future. We now stand on the farther side of Christ's life, death, and resurrection and have a perspective Simeon didn't have. I know what I say here will be misused by those who do not want to be involved in the ache and trauma of our times and will be turned off by others who believe the whole cause only has to do with this world.

But we need the counsel and caution of someone like Christopher Blumhardt, who wrote a century ago, "The social movement as we see it today still belongs to the world which will pass away. It does not represent the fellowship of mankind that one day will come through the Spirit of God." [5] For you see, ultimately, we are an eschatological people! We are a people whose final hope is future-oriented. Our *final* reason for being, the *fulfillment* of our hope, is not in the present, but in the future, not in the flesh, but in the Spirit. For "this too will pass away . . . "

Must we not agree with Blumhardt, at least to some

degree? "The attempt to carry my idea of God into earthly things cannot take root at a time when men are filled with the hope that *they alone* can create a blissful humanity." Ultimately—and you must be sure you read me clearly when I emphasize *ultimately*—our vision is beyond history. Finally, it is not a kingdom on earth we can create. It is a fellowship in the Spirit that acts responsibly in this life, knowing fulfillment comes in the timeless, when everything is under God's supreme control. This should give us an abandonment to act in the NOW in an even more courageous manner than our humanitarian contemporaries. To know Jesus Christ as the catalyst and confirmation of this conviction is to have your final perspective so sure you *can* celebrate history!

In the novel, *The Spy Who Came in from the Cold,* the Communist agent Fiedler is interrogating the captured English agent, Leames. He wants to know what motivates the Western agents to fight against Communism. " 'What do you mean, a philosophy?' Leames replied. 'We're not Marxists, we're nothing. Just people.' 'Are you Christians then?' Fiedler persisted. 'They must have a philosophy.' 'Why must they? Perhaps they don't know; don't even care. Not everyone has a philosophy.' Leames answered, a little helplessly. 'Then tell me what is your philosophy?' 'Oh, for Christ's sake,' Leames snapped, and they walked on in silence for a while." [6] For Christ's sake, indeed!

Are we nothing, anonymous, with no philosophy either we or others can identify? For Christ's sake we have a cause, a conviction, and a commitment to be agents of change and to celebrate history because of it! For God is in control in his world for a purpose beyond it, in us for beyond us, and in us for others for their hope in history—and beyond. If others discover it as we have, they will celebrate, too!

11
A Celebrating Community

For a number of years I've been experiencing a new
and thrilling experience in corporate worship on Sunday. It
has been in fellowship with people who have a common
sense of awareness of the Holy Spirit in one another, of
human and divine meeting, of mutuality of love and support.
I haven't felt this experience was commonly understood by
everyone present in the congregation, though one never
knows all of what is going on in the privateness of people,
and there are many forms and expressions of "celebrative
worship." The point is, celebration is vital to worshipping
God, and if a congregation is missing it, it misses an essential aspect of its being.

One religious art banner reads, "Celebration is offering
the creation and agony in this day to a transforming God."
I hesitate to be judgmental. But this statement seems a far
cry from what an outsider might observe of so many church
services. Passive people in screwed down pews regimented
row on row, listening to a professional, and half-heartedly
singing difficult hymns, do not seem to exhibit the life and
joy of God's people that throbbed in those first early Christians. It might have been entirely my own personal problem, but there were a few times in the past when I could
have screamed. I've talked with many who didn't scream.
They just stopped coming to church.

But is it idealistic to believe that those times most of us

107

have had, flashes of vital and spontaneous joy and power, moments of deep and moving life in a congregation gathered, should not be the continued experience of the whole congregation? Is it unrealistic to hope that whatever the denominational form or ecclesiastical mores it would become such a normal experience that people visiting would say, "Wow! These people have something I want!"? These moments should come in worship or on picnics, in study, in prayer, or at coffee-klatches. For the church is to be a celebrating community because we have something to celebrate about all the time!

Go back with me to the Parable of the Prodigal Son which we renamed "The Parable of the Elder Brother" (Luke 15:11–24). The youngest member of the family, one of two boys, has been away. We don't know how long he has been gone, but we sense it has been some time by the agony written in the face of his father. It isn't that the boy took with him half of the family assets, his future share of the inheritance. It is that he was immature and strong-minded. He wanted to find out about life and went looking for it in the wrong places. He wanted to "live," as he said. He was tired of the family and responsibility—the whole scene. He wanted to "split." So he had headed for the big city, his wallet bulging. Word had come back he was living it up all right! The typical misunderstanding of "celebration" had to be learned the hard way! He found out about "life"— all the seamier sides of life he had been protected from as a youth. He had ended up out of money, dissipated and scraping together a living doing something that violated some basic teachings and that even he felt impure in doing.

Then he was coming home. No one knew if he had changed, matured, or had learned anything from the wasted years. They just knew he was coming home.

And the father of the family, who had prayed and cried over the reports which had filtered back over the months— and often looked down the road leading from the house—ran, robe flying, arms flung wide, to welcome him home. Not a word of reproach, not a hint of sarcasm, not a reflection of the past mistakes and sorrow, the father hugged him to himself and *threw a party!*

Now, in using our holy imagination, let's broaden the story to make it applicable to us gathered as a church. For each of us is the prodigal son, and the father is God our father. Imagine yourself right now as the prodigal just returned and God as the father receiving you back. Imagine the fear of judgment draining out of you, the apprehensions of chastisement leaving. Imagine in your emotional make-up having felt separated from decency and destiny, from sanity and security, from faith and family, from love and real life. Imagine yourself having been dead, now alive again!

Then consider the joy you should experience, a feeling so great it's worth everyone throwing a party just to express it. The truth of the matter is, I suspect so many have united with the church for various reasons, under conditions which communicated something quite different from this, that they don't feel they once were lost and now have been found. They don't feel they have come home! They have nothing to celebrate! Naturally, they would not communicate joy to others either nor represent the church as any vital and deep reason for joy.

How can we help make the church a joyous experience, not only for ourselves but also for others? Well, *we will start by communicating to others this kind of happiness and we will experience it ourselves when we understand WE are the lost who have been welcomed into the Father's love and for- giveness.* We will catch immediately the significance of the father running down the road with open arms to embrace the son. We will realize it is God who has called us into his fellowship, who has embraced *us* in total forgiveness!

Further, we can rethink what is our true situation, and reclaim what we have, restore what should be, or create what should exist. For if we are to be the church of tomorrow, much less communicate the very life we each really want for our own experience, then we must listen to what others are saying.

One of the young college men of a former congregation wrote this to me:

The church as I see it is a formal, cold institution; it condescends and remains aloof from the people

. . . When one is in church, one must act stiff, formal, cold, and very self-righteous. . . . Too much emphasis is placed on the "role." Be polite, wear a smile, shake hands, and above all else, do not under any circumstances be yourself.

How can we hope to communicate, either with each other or with those who might join us looking for a sure sound of truth, if we live in the past like seminary students in a museum? I do not believe just jazzing up an old worship procedure with a few new gimmicks is creative worship. At a summer school for laity, someone reputed to be skilled in modern worship technique had been imported to kick off our day. It almost ruined the day for me. First of all, he looked as unhappy and joyless and self-conscious as any Victorian vicar. He ran us through some unfamiliar folk songs à la guitar, which no one knew and all struggled to follow. He used a few record selections which were less-than-enabling for communicating with the Lord. No, as alive celebrants of a living God, what will be demanded of us will be experiences which awake us to our senses, feelings, needs and history, plumbing what has been, is now and is coming.

Marshall McLuhan is now recognized as sharply tuned in to the age. He sees this as the age of "post-literate man." The Age of Writing has passed. We must invent a new metaphor, reconstruct our thoughts and feelings.

If the church dies and is born with every generation, what do we hold out for the new generation of the electronic, post-writing, beyond-book-and-print age? A hope that "they will come back," these youths who have vacated our church institutions and Sunday sanctuary experiences? Must we just try harder to indoctrinate them when they are young to accept the "Order of Service" and the good old hymns? Do we really care? I find all too many older people are more concerned about how they presumably feel in their own worship. Translated, that means going through the past familiar patterns. How many are interested in exploring the presently evolving age for authentic new expressions of faith in worship? But somebody *must!*

Probably we have all contributed to that image at one time or another, more or less. Probably at one time or another we also condemned those who seem to be polite and cold, formal and self-righteous. At the same time, fearful to be different ourselves, we were communicating the same thing to others.

Of course, we must define our terms, as the young college student who wrote me must also do. When are you "yourself?" I am thinking of that young fellow in our parable. Was he "himself" when he bolted responsibility and took the hard-earned savings of the family and left? Was he "himself" when he lived it up in the big city, tasting all the forbidden fruit? Was he "himself" when, as a result of doing as he pleased, he ended unhappily feeding pigs?

Apparently not. The text reads, "He came to himself." He woke up. He got in touch with dimensions of his inner world he had resisted facing. His values were reshuffled! He discovered back at home his true self and the true self of his father. The prodigal son discovered, not something new, but the love, acceptance, and reasons for a party which had been there all along. It was just new to him.

Our tradition has at its roots a celebrating community. Back in the first days we read in Acts of the Apostles: ". . . day by day . . . they partook of food with glad and generous hearts, praising God and having favor with all the people. And the Lord added to their number . . . " (Acts 2:46–47). Reclaim your real self as one who is to be a contributing part of a rejoicing people, a role meant for you all along. Loosen up and see what you can be as a free and released and joyous person.

We are also going to have to risk the danger of being a community of people instead of a group of private individuals institutionally associated.

You see, there is a danger of interpreting the Parable of the Elder Brother too simply. We could intimate that if we are all expectant and believing, we can come together as the church and always experience joy. Actually, the return of the prodigal probably meant more trouble. There was now another person to feed with half of what they used to have. He upset the hidden agenda and preconceptions of his elder brother. New relationships had to be worked out.

The church is all too often preoccupied with peace among

the brethren! This usually means freedom from conflict and not responsible relationships from honesty about feelings fought out in the form of straight talk. Preoccupied with comfort, we can miss the adventure of living.

Jesus could have told another parable as a sequel to this one.

> After the party was over, after the celebrating was through, after the servants had gone back to work, the older son sulkingly withdrew into an ominous silence. He did his work, shying away from conversation with the rest of the family. He avoided facing the family, which had the difficult task not to forget why they had the party and why they had such a responsibility toward each other—including the older son.

But now they could never go back! The significance of that celebration would be etched in their memories, recalling how easily they had taken each other for granted. Now they were to live in the dangerous, delightful, challenging adventure of community. That is what we are to be as the church.

Again, if we are to be a joyous, celebrating community, we must be adaptable and future-oriented. The devastating consequences of the party would have been for the boy to settle back into the old rut of previous relationships. But, as we have said, there was no going back. Of course, it would be just as devastating to try and manufacture a false *new image.* They could celebrate together in that family in the future when there was no party going on because of life together. At least they should. So should we!

I often wonder how many in the church really feel deeply a future-oriented life together. Too often it is the old ties that bind us, not our calling to service before us. Dr. James Smart reminds us that the most stubborn opposition Jesus had to his mission was from men who believed in God and were intensely religious.

"Jesus was not interested in numbers but rather in the shaping of a community of men and women who in their openness to the Spirit and Word of God would be really open to the future that God had in store for them.

"He turned men away who let themselves be bound to the past in such a way that they were not free for their future."

My God, though! How we are bound to the past! Aren't we? A Brooklyn pastor, Richard Neuhaus, is what I would call a practicing theologian who discovered an understanding of community in an unlikely place.

"Adaption, experimentation are essential. But we should not underestimate the power of the Songs of Zion. One night a number of us were in a dark, urine-soaked cell in the Brooklyn jail, arrested for having joined a sit-in at the office of the superintendent of schools.

"We discovered that one of the fellows had a Book of Common Prayer and we sang Evensong and chanted psalms across the cell block. We learned then what Hershel means when he says that it is more inspiring to let the heart echo the music of the ages than to play upon the broken flute of our own hearts." [1]

We celebrate a hope together, founded in the past, validated in the present in community together, and adaptable to whatever might come, open to the future. In fact, it is not just a hope we celebrate, but a fact. Paul says, "If for this life only we have hoped in Christ, we are of all men most to be pitied" (1 Cor. 15:19). We celebrate a person, Jesus Christ. For some it will mean trying to awaken new senses or thinking in new terms to feel. He stands in the middle of everything, making all things relevant. It is because Jesus is here that we can rejoice. That is what should make us different. That is what strangers should catch from being with us! Joyous, adaptable, future-oriented people, because all things belong to Christ.

But if someone not committed to our Christ is listening in, they might ask: How can you talk about being such a happy fellowship when the world is in such turmoil and there is such a crisis in the nation? Well, we must say this—*we celebrate something together that can only have significance if it has relevance for us when we are apart!* Let's continue to use our license of imagination with this parable. We might have to conclude that those of that family who could sit down together and talk about it (and probably the older son excluded himself from that conversation), would have to talk about the relevancy of some other issues. The discussion would have to include fair wages for their employees, living conditions of people in the community who not only had no fatted calf to kill for a party, but had no meat for their tables all month long, and a number of other concerns.

We will never have reason to be joyous and return week after week to the sanctuary expecting to celebrate all we have previously mentioned, if it is not tied directly to the stream of daily life Monday through the next Sunday. Sociologist Peter Berger is as disturbing to me as he should be to you. "The most common delusion . . . is the conviction of ministers that what they preach on Sunday has a direct influence on what their listeners do on Monday." [2] He is right, that there are reasons to doubt if what is said on Sunday really does have any impact on the life-style and value formations and decisions in the market place the rest of the week. It is a troubling thought. But its responsibility falls on both pew and pulpit. For me, I will continue to preach believing the Word *will* make a difference for me and my people the rest of the week!

So, if we piously sit in church and nod agreement to celebrating God's love for us and our neighbor and earn money from slum property, or spitefully use others, or destructively gossip about them; if we sing "Praise God from Whom All Blessings Flow" in the sanctuary and swear "By God, it's mine!" in our homes; if we allow the church to stand for the logic of equality, servitude and sacrifice, but live out in our business and social life a style of inequality, discrimination, superiority and selfishness—there will be no celebrating church fellowship. For the contradiction of our ways will keep a blanket of guilt and reservation smotheringly over us.

But if you will take God's love, justice, and mercy out into the world, then just think! God is throwing a party every Sunday—for you! He has run down the road, robes flying, arms outstretched, to embrace you and take you in! New and creative worship and relationship forms should communicate that! Why shouldn't our life together be a celebration?

But let your imagination go on further. Give it rein!

> For centuries we have been singing at the dedication of a church: "How awe-inspiring is this place! This is none other than the House of God! This is the very gate of heaven!" Today we sing these words in the rededication of total, integral, human society with all its art and technology. For this world is the very House of God. This is our gate to heaven. "How awe-inspiring is this place!" [3]

This is the community of faith loosed in the world! Alleluia!

12

Does It Really Work?

It's tough to throw the last chapter of your own book away! After writing the first chapters of this book, I went through a very difficult time. To save persons involved, I cannot share the details. But it involved my professional life and the direction of my ministry. It almost jaded my hopes and dreams, gifts and talents. Through it all I tried to celebrate! The convictions I have shared in previous chapters were tested again in the crucible of my own life. But I realized the *last* chapter I had considered for a conclusion at this point was of little practical help to me, as other chapters were expressions of very practical experience. It didn't relate to my situation. How could it help someone else? While the details of my own problems might not be the same for others, nearly everyone faces crises which take the joy out of living. You want to run away. You doubt your own worth. Things you have known and believed and have been successful in practicing in your faith come under question. It's natural to strike out against those who have upset your life, and you would like to call the fires of heaven down on them, as unchristian as you know that is. At the same time, if you are anything like me, you are sorry you can't please everyone and have everyone as your friend. You probably mutter, "How can I celebrate life when this is happening to me?"

Few people can shrug off this kind of an experience. Despondency sets in before you realize it. The mind starts digging up past failures, running them through the "computer" to see if they apply. It is as easy to reproach yourself over these failures as it is to be blind to any unpleasant truth about yourself that detractors might be expressing. But all too often they only bolster the wrong internal devices you already find operating, such as pride and self-justification. A few friends and loved ones have sound evaluations and constructive criticisms—if by this time you are even able to deal with them objectively.

So, does celebrating yourself really work? It sure does! I have found through all of this that I can continue to celebrate myself. The convictions I have shared with you in previous chapters work under the most trying tests. Thank God! They are not abstract ideas. And no one will be able to suggest that they apply only to tranquil lives lived in the ethereal realms of comfortable and pious, religious life. In the final analysis these processes have kept me not only celebrating but, I believe, have also kept me responsible.

Ralph Waldo Emerson might have taken it from Proverbs. "A man is what he thinks about all day long." Norman Vincent Peale makes it even more active. "Change your thoughts and you change your world." *First of all, I have tried to remember that I am what I think.* I know my subconscious mind takes my thoughts and programs them into every system of my being. How easy it could have been to succumb to those defense mechanisms and have been imprisoned in a hovel of self-pity. Just as easily I could have harbored mean and petty thoughts and become mean and petty. I find I must still work at not falling into these traps, for the process goes on. But it takes will. I am responsible for my thought world. No one else is. To admit otherwise would be to admit I was out of control. Only psychotics or severely neurotic individuals can be permitted such a dubious luxury. Some psychiatrists are now saying that even these emotionally disturbed people are capable of responsibility.

Someone has beautifully pictured Christian joy this way—"Joy is the flag flown from the castle of your heart when the king is in residence." *Secondly, then, I have not allowed myself to forget that Christ—and no other—is king of the interior castle of my being.* If that isn't a joy-creating conviction, what is? I have already shared with you my struggle years ago for freedom. When you have wrestled through all of those joyless attempts to run your own world and to measure up to everyone else's idea of what you should be, you discover how fruitless that is. I was once like the man Sir John Harrington described in "Of a Precise Tailor."

> He bought a Bible of the new translation,
> And in his life he show'd great reformation;
> He walked mannerly and talked meekly;
> He heard three lectures and two sermons weekly;
> He vowed to shun all companions unruly,
> And in his speech he used no oath but "truly";
> And zealously to keep the Sabbath's rest.

But Harrington doesn't tell us if the tailor ever found the joy of life, however much he reformed his style. I had not found it either. Then the spirit of the King came in. I don't ever want to go back to the time before that, worrying about everyone else's attitude about me, or fearing I am not religious enough. The Lord of life, the living Christ, the King is in residence within me! That is such a creative, dynamic, demanding conviction, I want to salute no other flag but the joy of knowing that—even though I forget it again and again.

Some people are surprised to hear me admit it, but I hate having *to give thanks in all things.* I suppose they expect some professional religious types, clergy and such, to practice all biblical admonitions perfectly. But it isn't natural to say, "I'm grateful, Lord, for this happening to me," when it seems your life is falling apart. Yet Paul knew what he was talking about when he urged the Thessalonians to do this,[1] knowing that if they didn't the Spirit would be suffocated within them. They would lose the feeling that God was in charge of their lives and working his will out, no matter what happened. So, I don't like doing it, but I do it. And again, it works! Even when I know I am rebelling inwardly to the pain and struggle I am experiencing, I am able to thank God for it. It has freed me from hating, and I have avoided resentment. It has often surprised me how a bad thought about another can give me a strangely "good" feeling I have had to avoid. Sometimes we really would enjoy a good case of resentment against someone. There is a perverted pleasure in thinking bad thoughts about someone you feel has wronged you. But it always returns, hurting you and preventing growth, real joy in your own being, or reconciliation with them. Hate and resentment poison their containers. You become negative and hateful. Talk about a quick route to quenching the spirit of Christ within—that is it!

What happened was that I was able to celebrate God at work in a very bad time of my life. I was able to see the celebrating life-style work in situations and in people. This is because Christ is Lord, not only of history generally, but also of my personal history and the history of others. I need to remember that truth, for that makes me accountable. So, whatever the events swirling around you with seemingly uncontrollable power, affirm God in the midst of them. Thank him and praise him that he is Lord! Jesus will bring a peace and an assurance you didn't believe possible. I know!

Here's the rub! We are touchy. I *might* be able to thank God for things in general when they don't look too bright. "But I draw the line when it comes to *that guy!* Pray for him? Not on your life!" You can theorize about loving those you don't have to like, but when it comes down to these very personal situations, it becomes quite a different matter. However, you can't rummage around in your Bible very long or walk very far with the Master before you have your answer. Jesus had a secret about growing up in personal power. He wasn't laying a martyr complex on us when he said, *"Love your so-called enemies and bless those who curse you and despitefully use you."* He knew that not only do we become what we think, we also transfer thought to others. If you believe someone should be different, especially more

loving and kind, stop judging. Become responsible for putting out thoughts toward that end. Visualize in your mind
that person *as* loving and kind. Thank God it is true. Claim
it! Believe it! Affirm it over and over. It will become true.
In so doing you will also discover how you must modify
your own attitudes, personality, and actions. For love is
healing not only to the one loved, but also to those who love.
For love thoughts are power. God's power! Didn't he say
he was love, and that the kingdom does not consist of words
but of power? It is remarkable to discover how it is possible
to love those who have tried, for whatever reason, to undo
you. It works! As one commercial on television used to put
it, "Try it. You'll like it!"

But I am also discovering how I must grow and change.
If we do not learn anything from events which happen to
us, all our energy and emotion is wasted. *I have determined
to grow in my character and spiritual life from this and
every situation.* That means *listening precedes talking.* Listening to God's spirit, to others, and to the actual events.
But it demands effort. For you have to listen over the pro-
tests of those devilish defense mechanisms which turn on
immediately to protect your ego. For they would insulate
you from learning anything about yourself. Sometimes we
will learn much more from those who oppose us than from
our friends. Have fun with your friends and learn from
your enemies could almost be a guideline. Obviously, because we do learn a great deal from friends also, it cannot
be a rule. But that is what I am presently trying to do,
learn and grow from those who have different convictions.
I've even been able to celebrate my "enemies." As a part of
that celebration I pray I can become a blessing to those who
are proving blessings to me.

Now, if I can get outside of myself long enough to approximate any objective appraisal of the situation, I can
see others around me have something to learn also. So many
people fail to see the more subtle implications of events in
which they are involved. People with deep feelings about
others often fail to notice that what they are saying and
feeling about another says more about themselves than it

does about the person they criticize or condemn. Read the Old Testament story of Job. It is so fascinating that you will not want to put it down until you have finished it. Job's friends not only could not listen to him—they couldn't help him. For they were trapped in the rigid convictions of their own ideas. So, they learned nothing from Job, failing both him and themselves.

It is very easy to be so caught up in your own problems that you miss people and their needs. More and more I am becoming aware of those around me who need to think for themselves about the implications of what has been happening. You find you are celebrating God and his use of you when you can get out of self-concern enough to be helpful to others. Asking a penetrating question can take people deeper in their own thought world. Today someone came up to me and looked me straight in the eye to get a reading. The question—how was I? It came out of true concern, not out of the normal superficial greeting this usually signifies. But I realized it was reciprocal. As he felt concern for me, he too needed to think about what he was experiencing. I was responsible to get outside self-concern in order to be sensitive to him also. The result was a much deeper level of mutual trust, for both of us, and for him the exploration of feelings he hadn't realized were bothering him.

Finally, I know more surely than ever before that celebration is not a feeling so much as it is an activity of my being. It is affirmation of what God has done for me and will do with me and through me. I celebrate the investment he has made in me in the past, even long before I existed, down through history. There is purpose to life. He is in charge, and I struggle again and again to remember and live as if that is true. For what I want tends to be easier, brighter days. It is so difficult to keep wants and needs sorted out. A couple of friends laid down the law with their children regarding materials for school. They were to make out a list of only those things they needed for the fall term. But they had difficulty getting the lists from the children. Finally the youngest, hedging, begged to at least go along to the store when his parents did the shopping. When he was told he couldn't go, he complained, "But how will I know what I need until I see what I want?" It is tough to admit you aren't much different from that child. But it is true. Knowing this in myself humbles me to pray my prayers differently. I know the Lord knows what I need much better than I do. I need to keep affirming him as a fantastic provider of all my requirements—and far beyond.

Starr Daily told someone I appreciate for his great insights, "Anything planted in the deep unconscious mind with love and prayer will come true. Nothing can prevent it!" I want to have my whole being filled with the conviction that life is worth celebrating. Not just life in general, but *my* life! Through love and prayer I intend to keep programming the deepest levels of my mind with affirmations that this is true. It will not fail.

One Sunday the Junior Choir was to sing, and I was to give a junior sermon but had forgotten to prepare one. We had a large oak tree in our backyard which I admired. It must have been two hundred years old and stretched a hundred and fifty feet or more toward sun and sky. Before leaving for church I grabbed a handful of acorns, asking God for a story. This is what he gave.

The first little boy in the pew was allowed to peek into my hand to see a miracle. Then I asked how many children would like to have a miracle in their hands. Every hand went up. When we passed them out, it came out exactly to the acorn! Then I shared the miracle secret. God had put an oak tree in each of those acorns. Once planted in the ground, with the warmth of sun and the nourishment of rain, a great oak tree could grow up to produce millions of other acorns—all out of that one acorn! Each of us is like an acorn. God has put a miracle in us—the possibility of his spirit. If we will allow it, that miracle can grow, nurtured by the warmth of the love of others, the nourishment of situations. We can grow up to not only live forever, but to produce many, many more miracles in the lives of others.

Isn't that a simple, profound, and beautiful story God gave? But it doesn't end there. After the second worship service a mother came up with her little boy. She said, "Go ahead, tell Mr. Cannon." Hesitantly he looked up with the greatest seriousness and said, "Mr. Cannon, I lost my miracle!"

How many have lost their miracles! But it need not be. We are what we think. Believe again that you are the most precious creature of all of God's creation. He has put a miracle within you. It is the ability to claim his Holy Spirit alive in you as the life that is abundant, free, and eternal! You can LIVE. Let your heart sing with the truth of that as mine does for you. I am celebrating, and I know you can too!

Notes

Chapter 1

1. C. S. Lewis, *Surprised by Joy* (London: Geoffrey Bless, 1955), p. 116.
2. Ross Snyder, "The Founding Ideas in the Register," *Chicago Theological Seminary*, Vol. 58 (May-July, 1968), p. 3.

Chapter 2

1. B. J. Cannon, *I Give Up, God* (Revell, 1970).
2. Cecil Osborne, *The Art of Understanding Yourself* (Grand Rapids, Michigan: Zondervan, 1967).

Chapter 3

1. Sam Keen, *To a Dancing God* (New York: Harper and Row Pub., Inc.), p. 66. Used by permission.
2. William Barclay, *Layman's Commentary, Matthew*, vol. 2, p. 169.
3. Keen, pp. 14–15.
4. *The Christian Century* (December 19, 1956). Copyright 1956, The Christian Century Foundation. Reprinted by permission.
5. For a creative and important treatment of gifts, see Elizabeth O'Connor, *Eighth Day of Creation* (Waco, Texas: Word Books, 1971).

Chapter 4

1. Editorial *The Christian Century* (September 24, 1969). Copyright 1969, The Christian Century Foundation. Reprinted by permission.

Chapter 5

1. Cf. the May 28, 1970 issue, *Life*.
2. Cf. the July 25, 1967 issue of *Look*.
3. Cyrus R. Pangborn, "Sex and the Single Standard" *The Christian Century* (May 17, 1967). Copyright 1967, The Christian Century Foundation. Reprinted by permission.

4. Father Clarence Joseph Rivers, *Celebration* (Harder and Harder, 1969), p. 12.
5. Ibid., pp. 10, 12.

Chapter 6

1. While this is true, segments of the church have been as discriminatory and racist as any other group in America, and we must be unrelenting in addressing racial discrimination wherever it exists in the church.

Chapter 7

1. William Pannell, *My Friend, the Enemy* (Waco, Texas: Word Books), p. 124.
2. Reuel Howe, *Herein Is Love* (Valley Forge: The Judson Press, 1961), p. 40.

Chapter 8

1. Elton Trueblood, *The Life We Prize* (New York: Harper and Row Publishers, 1951), p. 173.
2. Albert Day, *Discipline and Discovery* (Nashville, Tennessee: The Parthenon Press, 1961), p. 7.
3. Ibid., p. 8.

Chapter 9

1. Rivers, *Celebration*, p. 50.

Chapter 10

1. Edward B. Lindaman, *Space: A New Direction for Mankind* (New York: Harper and Row, Publishers, 1969), p. 154.
2. Ibid., p. 155.
3. Jeanne Richie, "The Unresponsive Pew," *The Christian Century* (October 18, 1969). Copyright 1969, The Christian Century Foundation. Reprinted by permission.
4. Harvey Cox, *On Not Leaving It to the Snake* (Toronto: Macmillan Company, 1965), p. 41.
5. "Who Are These Blumhardt Characters Anyhow?" by Vernard Eller. *The Christian Century* (October

8, 1969). Copyright 1969, The Christian Century Foundation. Reprinted by permission.

6. John Lecarre, *The Spy Who Came in From the Cold* (Victor Gollane, Ltd., © 1963) Used by permission of Coward-McCann, Inc.

Chapter 11

1. Richard John Neuhaus, "Liturgy and the Politics of the Kingdom" *The Christian Century* (December 20, 1967), p. 1642. Copyright 1967, The Christian Century Foundation. Reprinted by permission.

2. Peter Berger, *The Noise of Solemn Assemblies* (Garden City, N.Y.: Doubleday Inc., 1961).

3. Rivers, *Celebration*, p. 14.

Chapter 12

1. 1 Thessalonians 5:18.

Study Guide

Chapter 1.
Is Your Life Worth Celebrating?

Suggested Scripture for group study: Matthew 13:44–52

1. If you could characterize what your faith does for you, what word would you use?

2. Choose a color to describe your faith and explain why you chose that color.

3. When last could you say you really celebrated what you believe? How did you feel? How long did it last?

4. Name the kinds of influences which helped program or indoctrinate you in what you now believe. How much happiness and fun was there in it?

5. How would you describe the faith of your parents, and how did it influence yours, both negatively and positively?

6. Now, read the Scripture passage imagining sitting in a house with Jesus who tells you these parables. You know he is going to ask you directly, "How does this apply to your life?" Think about it quietly in the group. Then share what he is saying to you about this aspect of your life right now.

Chapter 2.
The Joy of Breaking Out

Suggested Scripture for group study: Matthew 11:18–19;
12:1–8
Galatians 5:1

1. Are you fun to live with? To work with? What do you believe are the major factors directly contributing to this?

2. What stereotyped image do others have of you? What *oughts* govern your behavior?

3. Who are the people with whom you communicate the most joy, freedom, and spontaneity? Is it with those closest to you? Who should it be?

4. When are you most spontaneous?

5. Are you ever spontaneous spiritually, religiously?

6. Fantasize for a moment. How could Christ, if he were alive and a spiritual presence personally known, make a person free and happy? What would have to happen for that to be a reality daily in the kind of world in which most of us live?

7. Describe the image of Jesus the Scripture passage from Matthew conjures up. In what ways does it stimulate a "breaking out" of some prisons in your life?

8. What suggestions does this chapter give?

9. Where are the suggestions most relevant to you?

Chapter 3.
Can You Celebrate Yourself?

Suggested Scripture for group study: 2 Corinthians
11:16–23
12: 1–10

1. What is your self-image?

2. Are you free to fail?

3. How do you handle success or compliments? How do you receive gifts?

4. What don't you like about yourself? Can it be changed? What part needs to just be accepted?

5. What ability, talent, or personality characteristic do you like about yourself and can rejoice in?

6. If you knew you couldn't fail, what would you do?

7. How free are you from your past?

8. If you were to define a growing edge of your being, what would it be?

9. Of the several suggestions in this chapter, which ones most apply to your life now? Which ones would you like to claim now? Will you right now?

10. Does Paul have an affirmation in this Scripture of you that you can claim? What prevents it? What would you like to cast aside? Can you do it now with the support of the group to pray for you?

11. Consider where you are in your spiritual journeys, and discuss if you want to declare any new and specific affirmations for yourself.

Chapter 4
How Can We Celebrate, Feeling As We Do?

Suggested Scripture for group study: Luke 10:41–48
Romans 8:1–9

1. What comes to mind when you think of your feelings? Play a word association game. Draw a large circle on a piece of paper and write ME in the center. Then write in the circle words describing both negative and positive feelings you generally have, each located in distance to the center ME according to how strong and active they are in you.

2. Do good or bad feelings tend to dominate in your experience?

3. Do you think of Jesus as being an emotional person?

(Do you make the mistake of meaning "over-emotional" for "emotional"?) Read the Scripture and inter-act.

4. There are eight Scripture verses and six suggestions in this chapter. Which ones speak most clearly to you? How do you propose going about applying them to your personal life?

5. Take a moment and ask the group for insights or affirmations as each one "stakes a claim" about these commitments.

Chapter 5.
Celebrate Your Sexuality

Suggested Scripture for group study: Matthew 5:27–30,
6:22–23
Mark 7:14–23

1. Rather than let this be either academic or embarrassing, with discretion deal with yourself and consider this as a leading question—How do you see sexuality as a natural part of your personality?

2. What has troubled you most about the overt display of sex in our culture on the one hand, but also the negative, suspect attitude of the church on the other?

3. Notice in Matthew 5:27–30 that Jesus uses the frames of reference of his day and speaks primarily to men. Do men and women lust for others in the same ways?

4. What is the distinction made regarding sexuality as a positive part of life? Give examples from your life.

5. How do you honestly relate to the opposite sex? How would you like to? What bothers you? Pleases you?

6. How have you felt about this chapter? When do you

believe it went too far, didn't go far enough, or missed you? Why do you think that was so?

7. Do you celebrate your own sexuality? Give examples.

Chapter 6.
Rejoicing in Your Brother

Suggested Scripture for group study: Luke 15:25–32

1. How much of yourself do you see in this Scripture passage?

2. What is most difficult for you in relating to the social misfit, those who differ from you in life-style, dress, decorum? Beneath the surface, what do you believe is the psychological cause of this difficulty?

3. What kind of person do you find it most difficult to affirm, relate to, try to understand, accept? What if you *knew* there were unrealized potential which could be released? Would that change your attitude or willingness to relate to this person more positively? Why?

4. Be honest now—must people fulfill your image of what they must be to be truly accepted by you? How much latitude are you willing to give? How much do you expect for yourself from others?

5. How do you like the title, "The Church for Losers"? Share, not what you think, but what you *feel* about that.

6. What could you do to make the church available and relevant to the lost, the losers, the lonely, and the unwanted and different? Is there some specific step you can share with the group which you are willing to make regarding this possibility?

Chapter 7.
Celebrating Through Preferring Others

Suggested Scripture for group study: John 3:25–36

1. Read the Scripture and picture John developing a following, disciples, and notoriety. Be quiet for a bit and think how difficult it has been when you have felt someone coming along pushing you out of some prominence or taking your place.

2. What bothers you most about this chapter of the book? Get at the *feelings* you have about this.

3. At what point do you feel the challenge could be most risky for you personally?

4. Give examples of where you prefer others over yourself. To what degree do you put qualifications on it? In other words, just how far would you go? Clarify where you feel confusion over celebrating yourself and preferring others.

5. Give a recent example of having had joy in preferring another.

6. How is it with you regarding the racial issue? Don't preach or make statements, but clarify where you can be most free regarding preferring those of another race over against preferring yourself and where you find limitations and prejudices within yourself limiting you from being abandoned.

7. How do you think Christ can help you move farther on in security, maturity, and love toward a new love-style he might better prefer for you? Where could you start practically?

Chapter 8.
Can Suffering Be a Cause to Celebrate?

Suggested Scripture for group study: Matthew 16:21–28

1. As someone reads the Scripture, think about your Christian discipleship. Has there been a time when you switched from just going along with it all and a specific decision when cost and service was demanded?

2. Clarify your understanding of the three phases of discipleship— (1) denial of self, (2) taking up your cross, and (3) following.

3. Be very clear about the difference between suffering brought on by ignorance and sin and suffering resulting from a good cause or holy obedience. Also note the difference between suffering from a natural problem and a cross which is laid on you because of discipleship. Also between redemptive and destructive suffering. Give examples from your personal life.

4. Do you have any example of suffering you feel came out of your own discipleship to Christ? Was there cause to celebrate? How might there have been?

5. What should be the results of such caring?

6. Where might this chapter speak most personally to your need, either in the present or in preparation for something in the future?

Chapter 9.
Celebrating Life Even Facing Death

Suggested Scripture for group study: John 16:25, 17:5
20:11–18

1. What is the most serious problem you have ever faced? What is it now? Has the person of Christ had any relevance for it? How? If not, has it been because you knew him but received no answer, strength, or power or because you didn't really feel he was present?

2. Can you thank God for trouble? How do you do it?

3. Do you ever ask, in trouble or joy, "Lord, what are you seeking to have me discover of your love and will in this?"

4. Do you feel uneasy about talking about death? What have you thought through regarding your own death?

5. Some people do not even make wills because they are unable to face the fact that they will someday die. Have you made a will? Are there any aspects of it which witness to your faith, to Christian values, to the on-going responsibility of Christian stewardship?

6. What one point, more than any other, has spoken to you in this chapter?

Chapter 10.
Celebrating History

Suggested Scripture for group study: Luke 2:22–38

1. Do you believe there is a divine purpose being worked out in history?

2. How much do you think events are in the hands of man?

3. Name the things in which you can rejoice today in the world. Where could you say God's purpose is possibly being executed?

4. Name the things in which you despair in our world which you believe could be different, which would serve God's purpose, if Christ's people acted responsibly?

5. Can you see yourself affecting history? How?

6. What role might Christians like yourself play in being used by God to effect his strategy for the world if you "got your thing together"?

7. Where could your church make a specific impact on

the course of events—to God's glory? Where is there social responsibility being avoided or missed? Read again Jesus' interpretation of his mission, Luke 4:14–30, and talk about its implications for your piece of history in the making in the community in which you live.

Chapter 11.
A Celebrating Community

Suggested Scripture for group study: Luke 15: 11–24

1. What personal emotion comes to mind when you think of the word "church"?

2. Name the last time you celebrated. Be clear about what the word "celebrate" means. Describe the feelings and how relationships were expressed. Now describe the last time you felt that way in your church. How could you put the two together?

3. Consider the idea in which a visitor says, "Wow! These people have something I want!" Is that ever true in your church fellowship? If not, why not? How might that be different? What part could you play?

4. What do you believe most prevents your church from really becoming more of a celebrating fellowship? What could you and your friends do to change it?

5. Name specific ways you might apply the suggestions in this chapter to bring it off.

Chapter 12.
Does It Really Work?

Suggested Scripture for group study: Matthew 5:20–24,
38–48
6:25–34, 7:7–14

1. How do you tend to react emotionally when things start going wrong for you?

2. How do you react to ideas of prayer, worship, gratitude, and thanks in these times?

3. What "got at you" most in this chapter?

4. If the thesis is true—you are what you think—what does your thought-world say about you?

5. What is the deeper implication for you at this time in your life that the King is in residence within you?

6. Tell of a recent experience of thanking God for a difficult or unpleasant time.

7. How about thanking God for an "enemy"—someone you don't like or who has hurt you? Is celebrating your trouble or your enemy an exception, an impossibility, or a normal part of your life? Give examples.

8. Where are you growing most in the areas of struggle, tension, or conflict with others?

9. Have you been responsible for what is programmed into your subconscious mind? Will you?

10. Have you claimed the miracle within you? Are you celebrating? Can you begin? Can the group make a covenant together to help support one another in areas in which each of you wants to grow?